# Guaranteed Formula for Effective Business Writing

by Everett Ofori, MBA
(Heriot-Watt University, UK)

**Guaranteed Formula for Effective Business Writing**
Copyright ©2017 by Everett Ofori

ISBN 10: 1-894221-10-9
ISBN 13: 978-1-894221-10-8

Author contact: everettofori@gmail.com
www.everettofori.com

(c) Everett Ofori. All rights reserved. No part of this publication may be reproduced, stored in a retrieval system or transmitted in any form or by any means, electronic, mechanical, photocopying, recording or otherwise without the express written permission of the publisher, except in the case of brief quotations embodied in critical articles and reviews. Printed in the United States of America and the United Kingdom.

As soon as you move one step from the bottom,
your effectiveness depends on your ability
to reach others through
the spoken or written word.

- Dr. Peter F. Drucker
Management Consultant, Professor, Author

✳✳✳

...though anyone can learn to write effectively, it takes hard work...writing is like any other skill — you can improve, but you'll have to dedicate yourself to it. The easier path is to settle for being a so-so writer...If you can write — really write — people will assume certain other things about you, the most important is that you're a clear thinker.

- Bryan A. Garner
Author & Distinguished Research Professor of Law
Southern Methodist University, USA

# Other books by Everett Ofori

***Succeeding From the Margins of Canadian Society: A Strategic Resource for New Immigrants, Refugees and International Students***
© 2009 by Francis Adu-Febiri and Everett Ofori
ISBN 978-1-926585-27-7

***Read Assure: Guaranteed Formula for Reading Success with Phonics***
© 2010 by Everett Ofori
ISBN 978-1926585833

***The Changing Japanese Woman: From Yamatonadeshiko to YamatonadeGucci***
©2013 by Everett Ofori
ISBN-13   978-1894221047

***Prepare for Greatness: How to Make Your Success Inevitable***
©2013 by Everett Ofori
ISBN-13   978-0921143000

***Guaranteed Formula for Writing Success***
©2016 by Everett Ofori
ISBN-13   978-1894221115

***Guaranteed Formula for Public Speaking Success***
©2016 by Everett Ofori
ISBN-13   978-1894221078

***The Global Student's Companion: 10,001 Timeless Themes and Topics for Dialogue, Discussion, and Debate Practice***
Compiled by Everett Ofori
ISBN-13   978-1894221023
©2016 by Everett Ofori

If you can think well, plan well, write well, and speak well, you have all that you need to change the course of human history, or at least, your own history.

-Everett Ofori

***Simple English is no one's mother tongue. It has to be worked for.***
- Jacques Barzun, American writer & educator

# Table of contents

| | Page |
|---|---|
| Acknowledgments | 9 |
| Note to Instructor & Student | 9 |
| For Classroom Use | 9 |
| Preface | 10 |
| Indispensable Writers' Resources | 11 |
| Reference Phrases - If Need Be | 12 |

    Salutation and Complimentary Close
       - When you do not know the name of the person you are writing to
       - When you know the name of the person you are writing to
       - When you are writing to a good friend
    Greetings at the Start of a Letter (A Warm Opening)
    Requests / Inquiries
    Responding to Requests / Inquiries / Orders
    Close (request-related)
    Asking for Help
    Possible Responses to Requests for Help
    Following a Phone Call
    Bad News Letter
    Good News Letter
    Expressing Sympathy and Condolences
    Apology Letters
    Asking for Information
    Complaining
    Asking for Payment
    Acknowledging Payment
    Payment / Reminders / Collection letters
    Congratulating Others
    Invitations (informal)
    Invitations (formal)
    General Opening Lines - emails / letters (mixed bag)
    General Opening Lines - responding to emails / letters (mixed bag)
    General Closing Lines - emails / letters (mixed bag)
    Rejection of Application

| | | |
|---|---|---|
| Unit 1 | Writing Styles: the good, the bad, and the ugly | 28 |
| | Fun with Grammar #1 | 36 |
| Unit 2 | Prepare, Write, Edit (PWE) | 37 |
| | Fun with Grammar #2 | 46 |
| Unit 3 | Grammar: Front and Center | 47 |
| | Fun with Grammar #3 | 59 |
| Unit 4 | YOU and ME | 60 |
| | Fun with Grammar #4 | 67 |
| Unit 5 | IDAC: Your 4-point Plan | 68 |
| | Fun with Grammar #5 | 78 |
| Unit 6 | IDAC: I is for Introduction | 79 |
| | Fun with Grammar #6 | 86 |
| Unit 7 | Common Errors in Business Writing | 87 |
| | Fun with Grammar #7 | 94 |
| Unit 8 | The Reader's Need: Revisited | 95 |
| | Fun with Grammar #8 | 101 |
| Unit 9 | Know Your Formats | 102 |
| | Fun with Grammar #9 | 109 |
| Unit 10 | Memorandum (Memo) | 110 |
| | Fun with Grammar #10 | 118 |
| Unit 11 | Writing Frameworks | 119 |
| | Fun with Grammar #11 | 127 |
| Unit 12 | The Paragraph | 128 |
| | Fun with Grammar #12 | 135 |
| Unit 13 | Sentence Variation | 136 |
| | Fun with Grammar #13 | 148 |
| Unit 14 | Getting Comfortable with Writing | 149 |
| | Fun with Grammar #14 | 162 |
| Unit 15 | Relevance | 163 |
| | Fun with Grammar #15 | 171 |
| Unit 16 | The Two-Handed Mouth | 172 |
| | Fun with Grammar #16 | 196 |
| Unit 17 | From IDAC to GIDAC | 197 |
| | Fun with Grammar #17 | 206 |
| Unit 18 | Good News & Bad News Letters | 207 |
| | Fun with Grammar #18 | 213 |

| | | |
|---|---|---|
| Unit 19 | Holding Productive Meetings: Writing Meeting Minutes | 214 |
| | Fun with Grammar #19 | 227 |
| Unit 20 | Harvard Referencing & Citation | 228 |
| | Fun with Grammar #20 | 233 |
| Unit 21 | Summarizing | 234 |
| | Fun with Grammar #21 | 242 |
| Unit 22 | Reports | 243 |
| | Fun with Grammar #22 | 254 |
| Unit 23 | More on Reports | 255 |
| | Fun with Grammar #23 | 264 |
| Unit 24 | The Incident Report | 265 |
| Unit 25 | The Progress Report | 271 |
| Unit 26 | The Memorandum Report | 279 |
| Unit 27 | The Trip Report | 288 |
| Unit 28 | The Briefing Note | 293 |
| Unit 29 | Writing a Proposal | 300 |
| Unit 30 | Count and Noncount Nouns | 318 |
| Unit 31 | Grammatically Correct Writing | 341 |
| Unit 32 | Additional Writing Tasks | 353 |

Answers to "Fun with Grammar" quizzes . . . . . . . . . . . 401
References . . . . . . . . . . . . . . . . . . . . . . . . . . 407
Recommended Books . . . . . . . . . . . . . . . . . . . . 407
About the Author . . . . . . . . . . . . . . . . . . . . . . 408

## Acknowledgments

Thanks very much to Ms Diana Camargo and Mr Frank Pridgen, who provided suggestions for improvement of the text. I am also grateful to all the instructors who have used this book in their classes and provided feedback on their experience. Special thanks to Mr Warren Buffett of Berkshire Hathaway, USA, for granting me permission to use an excerpt from one of his annual letters as an example. Students who have used this book have also provided invaluable feedback. Thanks.

- Everett Ofori, Tokyo, Japan

**NOTE TO INSTRUCTOR & STUDENT**

The instructor's role is to review the student's work for content, format, organization, and grammar. For best results, students should get in the habit of drafting their work, and then, reviewing the work themselves for common errors before submitting it to the instructor. The instructor checks the work and makes suggestions, pointing out areas of weakness and strength. The student might be encouraged to write another draft that incorporates the instructor's suggestions.

Answers to FUN WITH GRAMMAR quizzes can be found on pages 401-406.

The author highly recommends that this book be used in conjunction with an English grammar book so that the student can be fully immersed both in the review of grammar and the practice of writing.

**FOR CLASSROOM USE**

The material in this book has been successfully used in the classroom. Some students only have time for writing practice during class. Such students may read the material at home and do the exercises in class or read and write in class. Of course, it is also possible for the student to do both the reading and writing at home and meet the instructor for discussion and feedback. Ample space has been provided in this book for writing practice.

## Preface

Writing is a bit like swimming. You can imagine yourself swimming like an eel or diving to the bottom of the ocean like an octopus, but if you never get yourself wet, if you never experience both the dread and exhilaration of cutting through the water, you'll never be the swimmer of your dreams. If you want to be a good writer, you have to write…a lot…and get feedback from someone with the relevant knowledge and experience…and then write again…and again. It is the same formula that great writers such as Hemingway used to make their mark. Your goal may simply be to write polished letters and emails, but as with Hemingway, you will profit from repeated practice.

Here's an excerpt of an interview given by the Nobel Prize winning writer, Ernest Hemingway.

Interviewer: How much rewriting do you do?
Hemingway: It depends. I rewrote the ending of *Farewell to Arms*, the last page of it, thirty-nine times.
Interviewer: Was there some technical problem there? What was it that had stumped you?
Hemingway: Getting the words right.

Even for Hemingway, a native speaker of English and a writer besides, clear, powerful, and effective sentences did not come by magic. He had to work at it.

It might interest you, then, to know that this book provides over 170 writing-related assignments comprising emails, letters, reports, proposals, and sentence construction.

~~~~~~~~~~~~

*Write. Rewrite. When not writing or rewriting, read.*
*I know of no other shortcuts.*

- Larry L. King (U.S.A.), playwright, journalist, and novelist

# Indispensable Writers' Resources

**Dictionary**

Make it a habit to check and confirm the meanings of words. Some online dictionaries such as **www.merriamwebster.com** include an audio pronunciation link. You can thus benefit not only from knowing the meaning of a word but also how it is pronounced. Another dictionary that comes highly recommended is the Oxford English Dictionary.

**Thesaurus**

You also need to have access to a thesaurus, which gives you words of similar meaning . In fact, the online Merriam Webster dictionary includes a thesaurus that gives you both synonyms and antonyms.

One should be careful, however, in using a thesaurus because even though words may have similar meanings, often, they carry different connotations. So, choose your words carefully. If possible, the writer should confirm the specific meaning of an unfamiliar word before using it.

**Usage books**

Books on usage often focus on some of the more confusing words in the language. For example, what is the difference between preparation and preparedness? And what is the difference between continual and continuous?

Because of the similarity in the pronunciation or spelling of certain pairs of words, they are frequently misused or misapplied. Usage books aim to help writers make better choices about words and phrases.

Perhaps, the best known book of usage is *Fowler's Modern English Usage*. Others include John Sinclair's *Collins Cobuild English Usage*, and Michael Swan's *Practical English Usage*.

# Reference Phrases...If Need Be

The following reference phrases will help you to understand the patterns of language usually used in letter writing and emails. Use them only as a guide. Once you've come to understand the drift of English email and letter writing, let the issue before you dictate how you write the letter. Do not become a copy-and-paste writer. This book shows you a better way.

## Salutation & Complimentary Close
**(When you do not know the name of the person you are writing to)**

Dear Customer,

        Yours faithfully,

Dear Editor,

        Yours faithfully,

Dear Sir,

        Yours faithfully,

Dear Madam,

        Yours faithfully,

Dear Sir or Madam,

        Yours faithfully,

## Salutation & Complimentary Close
**(When you know the name of the person you are writing to)**

Dear Mrs[1] Roxbart,

        Yours sincerely,

Dear Mr Kobayashi,

        Yours sincerely,

Dear Mrs Widodo,

        Yours sincerely,

Dear Ms Thaber,

        Yours sincerely,

## Salutation & Complimentary Close
**(When you are writing to a good friend)**

Dear Eva,

        Best wishes,

Ray,

        Best wishes,

Hi Sandra,

        Best wishes

Hello Marcus,

        Best wishes

---

[1] You may put a period after titles (Mr. / Ms. / Mrs.). If you decide to do so, be consistent throughout. Don't use the period sometimes and omit it at times. Likewise, if you decide not to insert the period, then refrain from doing so throughout your document.

## Greetings at the Start of a Letter (A Warm Opening)

- I hope all is well with you.

- I hope you are enjoying the fine weather.

- I hope you and yours are doing great at this time of year.

- How are you? I trust all is well.

## Requests / Inquiries

| More formal | Less formal |
|---|---|
| I would be grateful if you could… | Could you please…? |
| I would appreciate it if you could… | Could you possibly….? |
| I would be most grateful if you could send me… | Send me… |
| I would be most grateful if you would… | Do me a favor, will you? |
| Would you be so kind as to… | Would it be possible for you to…? |
| I was wondering if you could… | I need… |
| Would it be possible for you to… | Could I ask you to…? |

I am interested in…
- *I am interested in the blue diamond that you advertised in the classified section of GemBright Times.*

I was interested in finding out…
- *I was interested in finding out if the blue diamond that you advertised is still available for sale.*

I understand that your company specializes in…
- *I understand that your company specializes in blue diamonds; I would like to obtain information about your products, including terms of delivery.*

I would be most grateful if you...
- *I would be most grateful if you would consider visiting our booth at the Milan Precious Stones trade fair in July, 20XX.*

I am writing with reference to your advertisement...
- *I am writing with reference to your advertisement in the Japan Herald of November 7, 20XX, for the services of a plumber. I am a highly experienced plumber.*

## Responding to Requests / Inquiries / Orders

Thank you for your letter of [DATE].
- *Thank you for your letter of August 1, 20XX.*

Thanks very much for your enquiry of [DATE].
- *Thanks very much for your enquiry of September 17, 20XX.*

I was happy to learn of your interest in...
- *I was happy to learn of your interest in our range of products.*

Thanks very much for your enquiry dated November 7, 20XX, in which you...
- *Thanks very much for your enquiry dated November 7, 20XX, in which you requested a copy of our latest price list.*

We are pleased to inform you that...
- *We are pleased to inform you that the product you inquired about is still in stock.*

It was a pleasure to receive your order for...
- *It was a pleasure to receive your order for 30 cases of Honey-Badger Cocoa drink.*

Thank you for your enquiry of [DATE], regarding...
- *Thank you for your enquiry of August 7, 20XX, regarding stylish mobile phone cases.*

We recently received a request from you regarding...
- *We recently received a request from you regarding steel-rimmed tennis rackets.*

With reference to your enquiry of...
- *With reference to your enquiry of July 2, 20XX, we have enclosed a product list and related prices.*

Our company specializes in the products you are looking for. We have therefore enclosed...
- *Our company specializes in the products you are looking for. We have therefore enclosed details of our full range of products and their prices.*

We are delighted to...
- *We are delighted to send you a copy of our latest catalog.*

## Close (request-related)

We look forward to developing...
- *We look forward to developing a mutually beneficial business relationship.*

It would be our pleasure to provide you with...
- *It would be our pleasure to provide you with any further information you might need.*

You can be sure that...
- *You can be sure that we will attend to all your orders promptly.*

Kindly let me know...
- *Kindly let me know if you need any further information.*

We trust you will find...
- *We trust you will find our quotation satisfactory and look forward to hearing from you again shortly.*

## Asking for Help

Could you...(for me)?
- *Could you prepare the report for me by Friday, November 7, 20XX?*

Would you please...?
- *Would you please let me know how the deal went?*

Would you mind (verb+ing)...?
- *Would you mind **coming** to the 14th floor, Room 1407, this afternoon for a meeting?*

Could you possibly...?
- *Could you possibly do a presentation some time next week on the research you have been working on?*

Would it be all right...
- *Would it be all right if the sales team held its weekly meeting in Room 5 this week instead of Room 10.*

I wonder if...
- *I wonder if I can borrow one of your trucks to move some goods from Buffalo, N.Y. to Toronto, Canada.*

## Possible Responses to Requests for Help

| | |
|---|---|
| Okay, no problem. | (informal) |
| Sure, I'd be glad to. | (informal) |
| Sorry, I'm busy right now. | (semi-formal) |
| I'm sorry. I don't have time right now. | (semi-formal) |
| I'm afraid I am unable to fulfill your request right now. | (formal) |
| I would be happy to accede to your request. | (formal) |
| It would be my pleasure to implement the program. | (formal) |

## Following a Phone Call

As we discussed on the telephone, here is...
- *As we discussed on the telephone, here is the price list you asked for.*

We were happy to receive your phone call yesterday. The...
- *We were happy to receive your phone call yesterday. The products you asked about are now in stock.*

In response to your telephone call...
- *In response to your telephone call, we are happy to offer you a small discount.*

## Bad News Letter

After careful consideration...
- *After careful consideration, we regret to inform you that we would have to withdraw our sponsorship of your soccer team, the Incredibles.*

Unfortunately, your request for...
- *Unfortunately, your request for special privileges to use the office from 1 a.m. to 4 a.m. is denied.*

Unfortunately, we cannot...
- *Unfortunately, we cannot grant you a raise at this time.*

Unfortunately, we are not in a position to...
- *Unfortunately, we are not in a position to extend the contract for your cleaning service into the next fiscal year.*

We regret to inform you that...
- *We regret to inform you that your application for a subsidy has been denied.*

I'm sorry, but...
- *I'm sorry, but we cannot accept the terms you offered.*

# Good News Letter

I am happy to say that...
- *I am happy to say that your application for admission to our three-month Executive Management course has been approved.*

We are delighted to inform you that...
- *We are delighted to inform you that your proposal for expansion of your territory has been accepted.*

# Expressing Sympathy and Condolences

It was with deep regret that we heard...
- *It was with deep regret that we heard of the death of your Chief Marketing Officer, Ms Lelani Delacroix.*

I wish to extend our deepest sympathy on...
- *I wish to extend our deepest sympathy on the loss of your son, Brian Busby.*

Please accept our sincere condolences on...
- *Please accept our sincere condolences on the passing of your mother, Mrs Laoko Brobbey.*

We were very sad to hear...
- *We were very sad to hear of the passing of your uncle, Mr Ronald Bokushi.*

We were very sorry to hear...
- *We were very sorry to hear that your grandfather passed away last week.*

## Apology Letters

I am writing to apologize for…
- *I am writing to apologize for the delay in processing your order.*

We are very sorry that…
- *We are very sorry that you received the wrong order from us.*

I'd like to apologize for…
- *I'd like to apologize for the delay in processing your order.*

I'm sorry about…
- *I'm sorry about the way our staff treated you and your family at our restaurant the other day.*

I'm sorry that…
- *I'm sorry that no one attended to you for thirty minutes when you visited our office last Friday.*

I'm very sorry for…
- *I'm sorry for the rude treatment of your grandparents at our establishment last week.*

Please accept my apologies.
- *What happened to you last week in our office was an isolated incident.* **Please accept my apologies.**

Please accept my sincere apologies.
- *Having to wait for so long for service is against everything we stand for.* **Please accept my sincere apologies** *and be assured that it will never happen again.*

Please forgive me for…
- *Please forgive me for the repeated mispronunciation of your name.*

## Asking for Information

I am writing to ask about...
- *I am writing to ask about the new training program you have created for new managers.*

I am writing to enquire about...
- *I am writing to enquire about your volunteering opportunities.*

I would like to know if...
- *I would like to know if I can take part in your art program.*

## Complaining

I'm writing to complain about...
- *I'm writing to complain about the way I was treated in your flagship store on Orville Road last Thursday, February 22, 20XX.*

I'm writing to express dissatisfaction about...
- *I'm writing to express dissatisfaction about the lack of air conditioning on your train from A to B on December 8, 20XX.*

I was very disappointed about...
- *I was very dissapointed about your misplaced attack on my secretary last Friday.*

I am not happy about...
- *I am not happy about the long, unproductive meetings.*

I am not happy with...
- *I am not happy with the long breaks some of you are taking.*

## Asking for Payment

Please see attached...
- *Please see attached an invoice for services rendered to your firm between February 7, 20XX and February 28, 20XX.*

We have enclosed our invoice for...
- *We have enclosed our invoice for services provided to your company in June 20XX.*

Our enclosed invoice shows that a balance of...
- *Our enclosed invoice shows that a balance of ¥15,000 remains to be paid.*

We would be most grateful...
- *We would be most grateful if you could send payment in the amount of $3,023.00 immediately.*

## Acknowledging Payment

We have received your payment of [AMOUNT] for [PRODUCT/SERVICE].
- *We have received your payment of $450.00 for services rendered in January 20XX.*

Thanks very much for sending payment...
- *Thanks very much for sending payment in the amount of $750.00 for the matrix-style solar lantern.*

# Payment / Reminders / Collection Letters

We hope you can send the funds...
- *We hope you can send the funds by the end of this month.*

This is just a reminder...
- *This is just a reminder that your payment for the piano is past due.*

We would appreciate hearing from you...
- *We would appreciate hearing from you regarding a possible payment plan.*

This is a friendly reminder that...
- *This is a friendly reminder that your payment for the scooter is due.*

Please let us hear from you by...
- *Please let us hear from you by December 2, 20XX.*

# Congratulating Others

Congratulations on...[OCCASION]
- *Congratulations on winning a scholarship to attend the International Business Management Institute's program on negotiation.*

- *Congratulations on your company's 10th anniversary.*

On the occasion of...we...
- *On the occasion of your company's tenth anniversary, we would like to express our hopes for your continued prosperity.*

## Invitations (informal)

Do you want to...?
- *Do you want to join the trek to Mt. Kilmanjaro?*

How about (verb+ing)...?
- *How about **joining** my work team?*

I was wondering if you would like to...
- *I was wondering if you would like to share the contents of the book with us.*

I wonder if you'd like to...
- *I wonder if you'd like to give us a demonstration of the product.*

There's a/an...[EVENT] on [DAY/DATE]. Would you like to go?
- *There is a motivational seminar on Sunday morning. Would you like to go?*

Would you like to...
- *Would you like to come to our office party tomorrow night?*

We're going to...Would you like to come along?
- *We're going to Ristorante Italiano Buono next Friday. Would you like to come along?*

# Invitations (formal)

It is with great pleasure that we invite you to attend our [EVENT]... at [VENUE] on [DATE].
- *It is with great pleasure that we invite you to attend our President's Lecture at the Tokyo International Forum on January 9, 20XX.*

I would like to invite you to...
- *I would like to invite you to a golf tournament that is taking place next month.*

If you have time, I'd like to invite you...
- *If you have time, I'd like to invite you to judge a speech competition.*

We'd be glad to have you join us...
- *We'd be glad to have you join us at the mayor's ball.*

Would you like to join us for [EVENT] at [TIME] [DAY/DATE]?
- *Would you like to join us for wine tasting at 7 p.m. tomorrow?*

We would be delighted to have you as our ...
- *We would be delighted to have you as our guest for a wine tasting session tonight.*

[COMPANY] cordially invites you to attend...[EVENT]...on [DATE]
- *ZZZ Company cordially invites you to attend our annual Music by the Beach event on August 5, 20XX.*

# General Opening Lines — emails / letters (mixed bag)

I am writing to ask about...
- *I am writing to ask about the coding job you advertised in the Friday, November 21st, 20XX issue of the Hong Kong Herald.*

I saw your advertisement...
- *I saw your advertisement for a bowling club manager in the Nairobi Times and I would like to be considered for the position.*

I received your name and address from...and would like to...
- *I received your name and address from The Business Connection and would like to find out if you are interested in collaborating with us in developing a new product.*

## General Opening Lines — responding to emails / letters (mixed bag)

Please find enclosed...
- *Please find enclosed a copy of our latest catalog.*

Thank you for your letter regarding...
- *Thank you for your letter regarding the Lightning Phone A1.*

Thank you for your letter of [DATE] concerning...
- *Thank you for your letter of September 8, 20XX, concerning the relocation of your office to Detroit.*

Thank you for your letter of...[DATE], in which you...
- *Thank you for your letter of January 7, 20XX, in which you asked about our company's latest invention, the XYZ Propeller.*

As stated in your letter/email of [DATE],...
- *As stated in your letter of June 6, 20XX, you wanted a copy of our latest catalog. We have sent it to you under separate cover.*

In reply to your letter of [DATE],...
- *In reply to your letter of May 7, 20XX, I would like to assure you that the meeting will take place as previously stated.*

## General Closing Lines — emails / letters (mixed bag)

| | |
|---|---|
| *I would be grateful for your quick attention to this matter.* | *I would be most grateful for your quick attention to this matter.* |
| *I look forward to hearing from you shortly.* | *I look forward to hearing from you soon.* |
| *I look forward to hearing your response.* | *I look forward to seeing you again soon.* |
| *I look forward to your reply.* | *I look forward with great interest to hearing from you.* |
| *I trust that you will give this matter the urgent attention it requires.* | *We look forward to building a strong business relationship with you.* |

## Rejection of Application

Thank you very much for your application of [DATE] for the position of... Unfortunately, we cannot...

> - *Thank you very much for your application of June 5, 20XX for the position of marketing manager. Unfortunately, we cannot offer you the position as it has recently been filled.*

I am sorry, but...

> - *I am sorry, but your qualifications do not meet the minimum requirements for the position.*

Thanks very much for submitting your application for the position of... Unfortunately, we do not...

> - *Thanks very much for submitting your application for the position of computer programmer. Unfortunately, we do not have any openings at the moment.*

# Unit 1
## Writing Styles:
## the good, the bad, and the ugly

*Your ability to communicate well will make more difference to your success in life than any other factor. No matter how much you know or how hard you work, your efforts will go unrecognized unless you can communicate successfully to others.*

- Jeanette Wortman Gilsdorf, Writer/Educator (USA)

### From fashion styles to writing styles

Over the years, there have been many different kinds of clothes fashion. You don't have to be a fashionista, someone who designs, promotes, or follows the latest fashions, to know that the classic style of fashion differs from the casual just as Harajuku style differs from Punk. And then, there are the traditional garments – the Japanese kimono, the Indonesian sarong, or the flowing robes worn in the Middle East. Each of these has a charm all its own. Writing styles are no different. They are not all the same.

### Writing styles

The kind of writing style favored in business today is the plain style. This contrasts with the style made famous by bureaucrats, often involving long words and long-winded sentences.

**Bureaucratese**: *Reduction of air pollution is a primary objective of the Fukuda regime.*

**Plain style:** *The Fukuda regime plans to reduce air pollution.*

Journalists write a lot. Pretty soon, they discover that they have to write some of the same stuff over and over again. They begin to use some of the same phrases again and again. These handy phrases, known as clichés because they are overused, make the journalist's job easy, but the writing is hardly fresh.

Here are a few clichés favored by poorly-skilled journalists:

- a storm dumped more than x amount of
- body of a dead man
- highly placed official
- in a surprise move

**Journalese**:
*A reclusive man, with no fixed address, unleashed a litany of insults and an unprovoked attack on a highly placed official. Amid a burgeoning crisis spawned by this event, the body of a dead man, believed to be the official, was found after a storm dumped more than 10 inches of rain on the capital.*

This kind of writing will not take you places. On the other hand, consider the plain style of one of the world's richest people, American investor Warren Buffett. The following is taken from Berkshire Hathaway's annual report for 2006:

*Charlie Munger – my partner and Berkshire's vice chairman – and I run what has turned out to be a big business, one with 217,000 employees and annual revenues approaching $100 billion. We certainly didn't plan it that way. Charlie began as a lawyer, and I thought of myself as a security analyst. ...I've taken the easy route, just sitting back and working through great managers who run their own shows. My only tasks are to cheer them on, sculpt and harden our corporate culture, and make major capital-allocation decisions. Our managers have returned this trust by working hard and effectively.*

Now, which part of Buffett's report did you not understand? He uses contractions (I've taken...), he uses commas, dashes, and an easy-going conversational style.

He uses short sentences, and simple words that are meant to express rather than impress. This makes reading his company's annual report a joy rather than the headache that many other reports are to read.

It is this plain style that you should seek to copy. Don't you want your readers to reach for your writing with the same sense of eagerness that Buffett's readers approach his reports? Of course, many people, including shareholders of Berkshire Hathaway, read Buffett's reports because of their interest in how much money he might have made them, but they must appreciate too, that they can easily understand his reports.

Even though Buffett <u>talks on paper</u> with his shareholders, his ideas are not simplistic; he writes about acquisitions, insurance, manufacturing, service, and retail operations, with the same kind of simple words that guarantee that you will understand his ideas.

Be like Warren Buffett – write in a conversational but respectful tone and your writing will be welcome everywhere. Indeed, ordinary words are best to make your meaning clear.

| **Instead of……** | **Write….** |
| --- | --- |
| Assist | Help |
| Commence | Begin |
| Close proximity | Near |
| Complete | fill out |
| Endeavor | Try |
| Forward | Send |
| Herewith is | Here is |
| Indicate | Show, Tell |

Even if you are not a native speaker of English, you probably know hundreds of simple words. It is natural to continue expanding your vocabulary as a learner of the English language but long, unpronounceable words are not the ones you need in order to write clearly. You need to expand your vocabulary, in part, because you want to understand what others write. Moreover, there are times when your large vocabulary would allow you to choose just the perfect word to express your meaning. Still, keep in mind that there is a lot you can say with the words you already know.

## Assignment 1

**(a) Rewrite the following badly-written passage in plain English:**

It is imperative for people engaged for the purpose of assisting a corporation in discharging its role to do so with absolute integrity. Furthermore, such individuals ought to have the full recognition that their contractual obligation with the aforesaid business entity makes it inexcusable not to employ their full powers in discharging their duties in exchange for the remuneration mutually agreed upon.[2]

_____

_____

_____

**(b) What do you understand by the advice, "Write like you talk?"**

_____

_____

_____

_____

---

[2] For one possible answer, see page 32.

## Possible answer to Assignment 1(a)
*Employees should work honestly for their wages.

## Shades of meaning: Using your Thesaurus
You probably have a <u>nice</u> friend, live in a <u>nice</u> city, make <u>nice</u> meals, and make <u>nice</u> with your colleagues. Words like <u>nice</u>, which we tend to overuse, lose their meaning and power to clearly express what it is we want to say.

If you look up the word "nice" in your thesaurus, you will find many other words that are close in meaning to it. Maybe, one of these other words fits better with the meaning that you have in mind.

If you are not sure about the meanings of the synonyms you find in your thesaurus, use the dictionary.

SYNONYMS (words with the same or similar meaning as another word in the same language)

ANTONYMS (words with opposite meaning to a particular word in the same language)

In the exercise on the next page, first find synonyms to NICE. Choose five of the words that come up. Then, find the exact meaning of each synonym and use the word in a sentence.

## Assignment 2: USE YOUR THESAURUS

|   | Find synonyms for NICE | a. Find the exact meaning of each word using a dictionary<br>b. Use the word in a sentence of your own |
|---|---|---|
| 1 |  | a. |
|   |  | b. |
| 2 |  | a. |
|   |  | b. |
| 3 |  | a. |
|   |  | b. |
| 4 |  | a. |
|   |  | b. |
| 5 |  | a. |
|   |  | b. |

# Assignment 3
## My Business Day (or A Typical Day in my Life)

## Prepositional phrases

Prepositional phrases can help you write in plain style because they often serve as substitutes to more difficult words.

## Assignment 4

| Prepositional Phrases | Form a Sentence with each of the Listed Prepositional Phrases |
|---|---|
| be annoyed with (someone) | |
| be annoyed by (something) | |
| apologize to (someone) | |
| apologize for (something) | |
| apply to | |
| argue with | |

# FUN WITH GRAMMAR #1
## Correct any errors you find in the following statements.

1) Yesterday, I have sent the parcel.

2) I am recognizing that the Internet is critical to business.

3) The Asian Tiger countries produces a lot of technology products.

4) Every February, we have went to Hokkaido.

5) Right now, I am not having any plans to take a vacation.

6) I brung some chopsticks with me.

7) Last week, he breaks his leg.

8) The business grown a lot in the last few months.

9) He speaked very well at the conference last month.

10) She wear a kimono to the picnic last Saturday.

# Unit 2
## Prepare, Write, Edit (PWE)

## Prepare

If you want to write well, sometimes, you have to slow down. Before you write, take time to think. Take time to prepare. This means considering why you need to write, who you are writing to or for, what information you need, and even what tone you should use.

## Preparation: Simple or complex?

Preparing may be simple if all you are doing is writing a letter to a friend to give information about an upcoming event. On the other hand, planning can take more thought and time if you have to describe the full range of your company's activities. There is a world of difference in how much preparation is required in the two situations. Preparation may be as simple as making a phone call to a colleague to confirm who is responsible for dealing with a particular matter. Or, it might be as involved as having to search through specialized databases to get some key information.

## Purpose

Before you start writing, know your purpose. Are you trying to answer a question or are you trying to persuade someone? Having a clear purpose can save you time.

## Know Your Reader

Knowing your reader is also important. How you write to your friend who is vacationing in Switzerland is likely to be different from how you write to the head of a big conglomerate that is considering becoming your client. The tone will differ. For example, if you are writing to the president of a big company, you might want to use a slightly more formal approach. On the other hand, if you are writing to someone and you know that the person prefers a friendly approach, it would not do to write a letter that is so formal.

Before you write, consider the following:
1. What's your reader's background?
2. What does the reader know already?
3. What does the reader need to know?
4. What are the reader's interests and values?

If you are writing to someone that you have never had any contact with, it is going to be difficult to know the answers to these questions. In that case, use your knowledge of the world and your imagination to create an image of the reader.

In any case, in order to have your letter taken seriously in business, it has to look and sound professional.

## Your Image

Pay attention to the kind of image you want to project. People who read your letters, memos, or reports will make judgments about you based on how you present yourself on paper or in other forms of correspondence such as email.

Image is important because, depending on your tone, your formatting, and even your grammar, you may come across as careless, thoughtful or inconsiderate.

Some might even read a letter or a note and decide that the writer is insincere. Your choice of words, what you say and how you say it, all contribute towards creating an image of you in the reader's mind. What kind of image do you want that to be?

# Organize

Organizing your writing can be useful to the reader. It can also be useful to you as a writer because it forces you to think more clearly about how one idea connects with another.

We cover reports later on, but you may have noticed that many reports are broken down into major headings, and sometimes, subheadings.

# Outline

A simple outline can be a list of points and sometimes, subpoints. Think also about the order in which to present the material.

Pay attention to organization, logic, and order.

# Email — Subject Headings

Do you pay attention to your email subject headings? If you do, you can help both yourself and the recipient. Writing a subject heading that is meaningful can help the recipient to decide how important the message is and make it easy to retrieve when necessary. A simple "Hello" in the subject line is harmless enough but it is not of much use to a busy person who is trying to figure out how to prioritize responses to dozens, if not hundreds, of emails.

Let your subject lines be short, meaningful, and free of filler words.

Here are some examples:
- Requesting input on social media strategy
- Potential collaboration on container housing
- Sales Managers: Quarterly Meeting this Friday

In all the email assignments in this text, be sure to include a subject heading.

# Assignment 5
**Write an email to a good friend explaining what you have learned from this unit so far. Encourage your friend to improve his or her writing.**

## Sorry, wrong question!

Someone might write to ask you about something but because of your greater knowledge of the issue, you realize that the person is asking the wrong question. In such a case, it would be proper to share with the person why you think another question might have been better.

You may answer the writer's original question and then show why another question might have been better.

## Rough draft

Writing an email, a letter, or a report, is not always easy. Even some professional writers do get stuck — sometimes for days! This is the famous (or infamous) "writer's block." Rather than staring forever at the blank sheet or screen and waiting for the perfect sentence to come floating in, why not just start even if the words don't seem to come out right? In fact, what you write at first does not have to be perfect. Think, plan, and write. Then, worry later about how to shape or reshape the piece. This is how some of the best communicators work. They do not seek perfection in their first attempts. In that sense, the process of writing can become an effective thinking tool. Your first draft may lead to a second or even a third attempt before you're satisfied with the tenor of your message.

*I write because I don't know what I think until I read what I say.*

- Flannery O'Connnor, American writer

## Editing

The newspaper articles and letters and books we read often seem perfect. In truth, some of the most respected authors, including Ernest Hemingway and James Michener, freely admitted to spending enormous amounts of time editing their works and even having others go over their work both for substance and style. Even for a short letter, consider going over it. You may find a typo here, a word that does not fit there, or still more, a sentence that could be shortened without losing the key point.

Editing can involve more than just checking for grammar. It can involve cutting out words or phrases or even an entire paragraph. It can involve rewriting parts of the piece or rearranging or reorganizing the order of the ideas you seek to present.

## Weaknesses

It helps to be aware of your own weaknesses so that you can pay attention to those areas during the writing process. Are you weak in spelling? Is your grammar a little rusty? If you know where your weaknesses lie, you can ensure that those weaknesses do not become a major handicap in your writing.

## Ordinal Numbers: Attention!

It's always disappointing to see someone write 2rd or 3th or 9st. Maybe, people make such errors because they do not know how ordinal numbers, which show the position of something in a series, are constructed. Here is a review:

| | | | |
|---|---|---|---|
| First | 1st | Sixteenth | 16th |
| Second | 2nd | Seventeenth | 17th |
| Third | 3rd | Eighteenth | 18th |
| Fourth | 4th | Nineteenth | 19th |
| Fifth | 5th | Twentieth | 20th |
| Sixth | 6th | Twenty-first | 21st |
| Seventh | 7th | Twenty-second | 22nd |
| Eighth | 8th | Twenty-third | 23rd |
| Ninth | 9th | Twenty-fourth | 24th |
| Tenth | 10th | Twenty-fifth | 25th |
| Eleventh | 11th | Twenty-sixth | 26th |
| Twelfth | 12th | Twenty-seventh | 27th |
| Thirteenth | 13th | Twenty-eighth | 28th |
| Fourteenth | 14th | Twenty-ninth | 29th |
| Fifteenth | 15th | Thirtieth | 30th |

# Assignment 6: USE YOUR THESAURUS

| | Find synonyms for RECEIVE | a. Write down the exact meaning (use a dictionary) <br> b. Use the word in a sentence of your own |
|---|---|---|
| 1 | | a. |
| | | b. |
| 2 | | a. |
| | | b. |
| 3 | | a. |
| | | b. |
| 4 | | a. |
| | | b. |
| 5 | | a. |
| | | b. |

## Assignment 7

You have just heard that an overseas-based colleague of yours, Peter Tamachu, has come to the city/town in which you live and will stay for a week. You are wondering if he will have time to get together for lunch or coffee.

Send him an email to find out if this might be possible. Let him know what might be a good time for you. Keep in mind that Peter is in your city for business.

## Assignment 8

Your company is considering translating a number of documents from one language to another. These would be made available to the company's overseas branches. Find out from Fancy Footwork Translations (Email: fftrans@bizcanada.com) how much it would cost (10 pages) along with other details such as turnaround.

# FUN WITH GRAMMAR #2
## Correct any errors in the following sentences.

1. After she write the article, I will send it to the editor.

2. Before he leaves, we will visits the zoo.

3. After we ate last night, we go immediately to the meeting.

4. Tomorrow, I will prepare some slides for boss.

5. By the time I finishing the project, she would have returned.

6. If you want to know more you must reading more.

7. You can meeting interesting people anywhere you go.

8. Right now, the boss doze in his office.

9. Currently, I'm read a book by Inazo Nitobe.

10. Have you see the latest Harry Potter movie?

# Unit 3
## Grammar: Front and Center

Below are some common grammatical errors: sentence fragments, run-on sentences, and the comma splice. A review of this section will help you eliminate these kinds of mistakes. Meanwhile, continue to be a diligent student of grammar.

## Sentence Fragments

A sentence fragment is a group of words that is presented as a sentence but falls short of the label because it lacks one or more key ingredients of a sentence. An actual sentence, according to the Merriam Webster dictionary is "a group of words that makes a statement, asks a question, or expresses a command, wish or exclamation."

The word 'fragment' refers to "a part" and is thus incomplete.
Here is an example:

*Not gone.*

The above is an example of a sentence fragment. What is not gone? The two words could be a part (a fragment) of a sentence but by themselves they do not make much sense.

In fairness, novelists and newspaper article writers sometimes use sentence fragments to achieve certain effects. Such writers are aware of when and why they should not use fragments. When they choose to use fragments, they may have a good reason to do so. If you study grammar well enough, you may also decide that in some of your writings you will include a fragment. As long as you know what you are doing, that is all right.

Consider also, that, while sentence fragments may be all right in a novel, in the business world, you do not want to appear too casual to the point of being perceived as careless. So in business, you might want to avoid using sentence fragments.

## Run-on sentences

With a run-on sentence, two or more independent clauses are joined but without the correct punctuation. For example,

> *We are going to the pool we shall eat hamburger there.*

In the above there are two sentences, not one.

When you have a sentence that lacks the correct break such as a comma, semicolon, or period, you have a run-on sentence.

With the proper punctuation, the problem of run-on is easily solved.

> *We are going to the pool, and we shall eat hamburger there.*
> *We are going to the pool; we shall eat hamburger there.*

Sometimes the run-on sentence may come about not because your grammar is poor but because you were in a hurry and simply missed putting in the proper punctuation mark.

Review your writing.

## The Comma Splice

When two independent clauses are separated by a comma instead of a period or a semi-colon, this is called a comma splice. This is sometimes deliberately used by novel writers, but some people frown upon such usage.

Here are some examples of the comma splice:

    a) *The wolf stood in the garden, the cat stayed in the tree.*

In the above, the two parts are better separated by a period or a semicolon. Instead, they are separated by a comma.

    b) *The company makes electronic gadgets, the company also makes beauty products.*

Here are some possibilities for fixing the above:

a)   *The wolf stood in the garden, and the cat stayed in the tree.*
     *The wolf stood in the garden; the cat stayed in the tree.*
     *The wolf stood in the garden. The cat stayed in the tree.*

b)   *The company makes electronic gadgets; the company also makes beauty products.*

     *The company makes electronic gadgets, and it also makes beauty products.*

     *The company makes electronic gadgets. The company also makes beauty products.*

     *The company makes electronic gadgets. It also makes beauty products.*

# Assignment 9
**Write an email to a good friend explaining what you have learned from this unit so far. Encourage your friend to improve his or her writing.**

# Parallel structure

------------------------------------------------------------

------------------------------------------------------------

Above, you see two lines that are parallel to each other. The lines extend in the same direction. In graphic arts and in mathematics, such parallel lines are considered pleasing to the eye. In both writing and speaking, we can use parallelism to add a bit of flavor to what may otherwise be boring writing.

*I want a cat. I want a dog. I enjoy swimming in the pool.*

In the above, the first two sentences are parallel while the pattern of the third is different.

*I enjoy eating sushi. I enjoy drinking juice. I enjoy dancing salsa.*

This works better as the three sentences follow the same pattern.

Many notable writers and speakers have used parallelism to good effect, including Canadian writer Margaret Atwood and United States presidents Abraham Lincoln and Barack Obama. It is not only in the field of politics where you can spice up your language with parallelism. You can use parallelism in your letters, memos, incident reports, and other correspondence.

Examples:
*We are going to dig the ditches, install the piling, and build the structure.*

*Some stood, others sat; some cheered, others cried.*

*We shall hire creative people, design great products, and provide terrific service to our customers.*

## Conciseness

Why use a hundred words to say something when you can say the same thing in twenty? Being concise means using only a few appropriate words to express your meaning.

## Semicolon

The semicolon poses a problem for many writers. Consider this: You have two sentences (actually independent clauses). Each of them can stand on its own but there is a relationship between the two. In such a case, you can use a semicolon to separate them. For example:

*My friend has two pets. One is a dog; the other is a cat.*
*She is Roman Catholic; he is Protestant.*
*The top floor office is huge; the ground floor office is small.*

## Quotation marks

When you cite someone else's words in writing, it is standard practice to put those words in quotation marks. This is a signal that the words are not your own. Here's an example:

*The principal said, "You must come to school on time tomorrow. I will have something very special for you all."*

## Paraphrase

If you borrow ideas from someone and you change the words of the original work, that kind of treatment does not use quotation marks. Likewise, when you report what someone else said in your own words, you do not need to use quotation marks. In such cases, you just mention the name or title of the writer or speaker as having been the source of the idea.

*The principal told us to go to school on time the following day and that she would have something very special for us all.*

# Apostrophe

We generally use the apostrophe to show possession, that something belongs to someone or something.

*The dog's breakfast.*

*The teacher's pet.*

When it comes to the third person singular (it), however, we write:

*The dog wagged **its** tail.* <= [Note that there is no apostrophe]
*The dog wagged **it's** tail.* = [The dog wagged **it is** tail] <= this does not make sense

***It's*** *hot in here.* [This is a contraction of 'It is" — in this case, the use of the apostrophe is correct.]

# Verbs

Whenever possible, use verbs. They strengthen your writing.

| Instead of... | Write... |
|---|---|
| Sakamoto is the winner of last week's marathon. | Sakamoto **won** last week's marathon. |
| There are so many cherry trees in Japan. | Japan **abounds** in cherry trees. |

# Assignment 10

Form sentences with the verbs below.

1. accomplish: _____

2. adapt: _____

3. assess: _____

4. authorize: _____

5. brief: _____

6. budget: _____

7. ascertain: _____

8. arrange: _____

9. assist: _____

10. author: _____

_____

11. calculate: _____

_____

12. analyze: _____

_____

13. advocate: _____

_____

14. advise: _____

_____

15. advance: _____

_____

16. acquire: _____

_____

17. expect: _____

_____

18. achieve: _____

_____

19. enshrine: _____

_____

# Assignment 11
**Write an email to a friend and explain what you have learned from pages 51 to 53.**

# Hyphen

When we use two or more words as a unit to modify a noun or pronoun, we hyphenate the two-word unit. In this case **two-word** is a modifying unit. Here are a few examples:

***one-way*** road / ***fresh-faced*** youth / ***eager-eyed*** soldier / ***two-tier*** system

# Spelling

In this age of spell-check on every computer, we should not be making too many spelling errors. Take time to go over your work and correct any errors.

Also, don't forget that the spell-check function cannot pick up words that are spelled correctly but do not fit the meaning you had in mind.

If you are not sure about a word, check the meaning to be sure that you are using the correct one. It is not uncommon to find reputable organizations writing ***principle***, for example, instead of ***principal*** or vice versa.

# Use Active Sentences

In an active sentence, the subject does the action of the verb.

> *The sales director visited all the local branches.*

The passive sentence does not focus on the doer of an action.

> *All the plants in the lobby were watered.*

Use active sentences as much as possible. You might find occasion to use passive sentences, but the active sentence is much more forceful.

## Assignment 12
**Write an email to a friend explaining what you have learned about the importance of verbs, the use of the hyphen, and spelling.**

# FUN WITH GRAMMAR #3
## Choose which of the two italicized words is correct.

1. The clerk **poured/pored** over the document.

2. The supermarket **isle/aisle** was full of carts.

3. On our visit to Morocco, we went to a **bizarre/bazaar**.

4. The marketing manager **broached/brooched** the subject of social media to the CEO.

5. Telemarketing can be a **compliment/complement** to other forms of advertising.

6. If you **flaunt/flout** too many rules on the job, you will be let go.

7. The president spoke in a monotone; I was so **boring/bored**.

8. Many accidents are **prevention/preventable**.

9. Everybody wants to **success/succeed**.

10. Sometimes, businesspeople have to be **patent/patient**.

# Unit 4
## YOU and ME

You probably work hard. You probably want whatever advantage you can get in life. You probably do not mind retiring early or taking a couple of vacations every year. Your life is important to you and you probably think a lot about how to make your life sweeter, better, more comfortable, and less stressful.

When you are writing letters or emails, please keep in mind that just as you worry about things that affect your life, others may similarly worry about the things that touch their own lives.

If you are writing to others in the hope of getting their cooperation, it would be a mistake to focus only on your needs. People are more likely to respond well to you if they know that you care about them and their needs or concerns.

A "YOU" oriented approach, therefore, will win you more friends and help you better influence business associates than an "I, ME, MY, or MINE" centered approach. Read the following two letters and determine which is more likely to get the desired results.

## SAMPLE LETTER A:

Dear Dr Mococan:

My name is Tomohiro Ogawa and I work for a pharmaceutical company in Tokyo, Japan. I have made some incredible advances in the field of influenza research and I am often told that I am destined for greatness, and that I might even win the Nobel Prize in the near future. Honestly speaking, I don't pay much attention to that.

Anyway, I am interested in learning more about the technique you pioneered, the Mococan Influenza Assay. I am working on a paper now that will be presented at a conference in Linz, Austria, in the coming year. I need to talk about your method briefly but I confess that I am not as clear about the details as I should. As such, any materials you can send me, including articles you have written, chapters of books, pamphlets, or personal notes, etc., would be greatly appreciated.

I look forward to hearing from you soon.

Yours truly,


Tomohiro Ogawa


## SAMPLE LETTER B:

Dear Dr Mococan:

I note with great interest your many superb contributions to the field of pharmaceutical research in general and influenza research in particular.

One of the techniques you pioneered, the Mococan Influenza Assay, is of great interest to my company. We understand, however, that it is proprietary; we would, therefore, like to seek your permission to apply the methodology in our research. As such, if there are any conditions attached to the use of the Mococan Influenza Assay, kindly inform us at your earliest possible convenience.

Your leadership in the field of pharmaceutical research is a great inspiration to me and the other members of my team.

We look forward with great interest to hearing from you.

Sincerely,


Tomohiro Ogawa

**COMMENTS ON THE TWO LETTERS**

What did you like or dislike about each of the two letters? Which has a better likelihood of getting the desired results?

## To write for results:
- Think "YOU"
- Avoid too much "I, Me, My, or Mine"

- Offer sincere compliments
- Show that you know something about the recipient (something positive, that is)

- Be considerate of the other person's time
- Use respectful language

- Avoid showing off
- Avoid wasting the reader's time with irrelevant points

# Assignment 13

| Prepositional Phrases | Form a Sentence with each of the Listed Prepositional Phrases |
|---|---|
| Be associated with | |
| Be aware of | |
| Believe in | |
| Blame for | |
| Be blessed with | |
| Be bored with | |
| Be bored by | |
| Be capable of | |
| Care about | |
| Care of | |

# Assignment 14

Your company is holding a workshop and lecture series on Saturday, November 7, 20XX. You need a lectern but you are unable to buy or rent one. One of your affiliate companies, which is two blocks away from your office, has a lectern that you want to borrow. The General Manager is Ms Kirsten Kardalian. Send an email requesting the use of the lectern; mention when you would like to pick it up and when you would return it.

# Assignment 15
## Form sentences with the verbs below.

1. identify: _____

_____

2. immigrate: _____

_____

3. emigrate: _____

_____

4. include: _____

_____

5. devise: _____

_____

6. industrialize: _____

_____

7. inquire: _____

_____

8. install: _____

_____

9. insure: _____

_____

10. journey: _____

11. reason: _____

12. overdo: _____

13. lament: _____

14. project: _____

15. pace: _____

16. notify: _____

17. manipulate: _____

18. master: _____

19. appoint: _____

# FUN WITH GRAMMAR #4
## Subject-Verb Agreement

**Fill in the blanks with the correct form of the word in parentheses.**

1. The sky _____ blue. *(be)*

2. Jamie always _____ to the gym after work. *(go)*

3. Baby seals _____ cute. *(be)*

4. Office ladies _____ Hello Kitty. *(adore)*

5. The chef _____ chocolate pie every week. *(make)*

6. The chef's apprentice _____ blueberry scones last week. *(make)*

7. Few babies _____ thirty-two teeth. *(have)*

8. I have _____ that guy since elementary school. *(know)*

9. They _____ a lot of mangoes every year. *(eat)*

10. She _____ late into the night each day. *(work)*

# Unit 5
## IDAC : Your 4-point Plan

British writing consultant Shirley Taylor, suggests a 4-point plan for writing that can work as well for letters as for emails: IDAC.

IDAC[3]

| I | INTRODUCTION | Give your reason for writing<br>Refer to the letter you are about to reply to |
|---|---|---|
| D | DETAILS | Give information and ask for all relevant information |
| A | ACTION | Mention expected response date<br>Mention when you want to meet |
| C | CLOSE | Sign off |

## Use of IDAC

For most emails and letters, it is possible to use the four-step formula (IDAC) to either write or respond. IDAC begins with an **Introduction**, which tries to capture the main point you want to make. Then follows **Details**, in which you present in-depth information on the subject. The **Action** part is for decisions such as meeting the person you are corresponding with, asking for a follow-up phone call or email, or in fact, anything that requires action on your part, on the part of the addressee, or on someone else's part. Finally, there is the **Close**, which you should keep simple.

---

[3] Shirley Taylor, *Model Business Letters, E-mails, and Other Business Letters,* Pearson, UK, 2012.

Here's an example:

|  | Dear Ms Yvonne Motozuki: |
|---|---|
| **Introduction** | We have received your request for a new credit card for your seven-year-old son. |
| **Details** | Newly-released policy guidelines from our headquarters prohibit us from issuing credit cards to children under the age of twelve. Even though you have been a longstanding client, we are, unfortunately, unable to fulfill this request. |
| **Action** | You may want to apply for the Junior Debit Card, which was issued early this year, and has become popular with parents who want to teach their children financial responsibility. If you are interested, please give me a call anytime on weekdays between 9 a.m. and 12 noon. |
| **Closing** | I look forward to hearing from you.<br><br>Sincerely,<br><br>Peter Samarama<br>Special Customer Accounts |

## Sample Apology Letter

    Dear Ms Leila Sayuri:

I:     I would like to apologize for the delay in dispatching the 35 replacement wheel covers that you ordered on November 2, 20XX.

D:     We have ordered them and our tracking system shows that there was an error in the shipper's data, which has caused the delay.

A:     Ms Sayuri, be assured that you will receive the hubcaps, No. 345, by Friday, December 7, 20XX.

C:     Kindly accept our apologies for any inconvenience caused.

    Sincerely,

    Kenichi Ogasawara
    Senior Logistics Manager

## IDAC – Just a Guideline, not a Commandment

As useful as IDAC is, there may be times when you find that you can present your message without covering all the elements of IDAC. Maybe, you will find need at some point to combine the details and the action or combine the introduction and the details.

In the following sample collection letters, does the writer observe IDAC?

# Sample Collection Letters

## REMINDER 1

November 16, 20XX

Dear Ms Janet Machado,

We hope that the 1000 20XX Acura model MDX K & N Air Filters (Gauze) that we shipped to you were all satisfactory.

You agreed to make payment by November 15, 20XX; this is a reminder in case there was an oversight.

Please disregard this message if you have transferred the funds into our account.

Sincerely,


Majime Ohara
Accounts Manager

## REMINDER 2

December 16, 20XX

Dear Ms Janet Machado,

Please note that we have still not received payment for the 1000 20XX Acura model MDX K & N Air Filters (Gauze) that we shipped to you in October 20XX.

You agreed to make payment by November 15, 20XX.

Enclosed is our account information.

If by chance, you have already paid, please disregard this letter and accept our apologies.

Sincerely,

Majime Ohara

Accounts Manager

# REMINDER 3

January 16, 20XX

Dear Ms Janet Machado,

Our records show that payment for the 1000 20XX Acura model MDX K & N Air Filters (Gauze) that we shipped to you in October 20XX is over 60 days past the agreed-upon payment date.

Our policy requires that we refer you to a collection agency, which we are reluctant to do.

Please pay within the next 10 days otherwise we will have no choice but to refer your account for collections.

We trust that you will attend to this matter with the utmost urgency.

Sincerely,


Majime Ohara
Accounts Manager

# SAMPLE ESTIMATE LETTER

Dear Mr Rowan Atkingan:

Please find enclosed the estimate you recently requested on XXXX parts.

| Product | Number | Quantity | Price | Quantity X Price |
|---|---|---|---|---|
| XXXX | | | | |

This quote is valid until December 15, 20XX.

If you have any questions please contact us, and we will respond without delay.

Sincerely,

Junko Nishi
Sales Executive

# Assignment 16
**Write an email to a friend explaining what you have learned from this unit so far.**

# Assignment 17

You met someone called Letitia Azuma at an industry conference; you think you could be of mutual help to each other professionally. Send her an email expressing how happy you are to have met her. Share your hopes for this professional relationship.

# Assignment 18

Your company has hired a new head for the IT department. You are busy, so you will not be able to meet him for a while. Send an email welcoming this new hire, Mr Mitara Lokko, to your company. You want Mr Lokko to know who you are and perhaps how you might work together in the future.

# Assignment 19
## Form sentences with the verbs below.

1. lease: _____

2. overwrite: _____

3. package: _____

4. pattern: _____

5. perceive: _____

6. overcome: _____

7. outwit: _____

8. light: _____

9. litigate: _____

10. persuade: _____

_____

11. personalize: _____

_____

12. enter: _____

_____

13. opine: _____

_____

14. officiate: _____

_____

15. reap: _____

_____

16. rear: _____

_____

17. conspire: _____

_____

18. prove: _____

_____

19. preside: _____

_____

# FUN WITH GRAMMAR #5

**Choose the correct answer from each pair of italicized words.**

1. The United Nations **is/are** working to make the world a peaceful place.

2. The United States **is/are** still a leader in world affairs.

3. Five hours of sleep **is/are** not enough for me.

4. The Irish **love/loves** coffee.

5. Japanese **is/are** the language of my heart.

6. One and one **is/are** two.

7. Five dollars **are/is** enough to buy a bowl of noodles.

8. The police **is/are** good at giving directions.

9. The news this morning **is/are** not good.

10. Linguistics **is/are** interesting.

# Unit 6
## IDAC: I is for Introduction

It is not always easy to grab a reader's attention and hold it. In writing an email or a letter, your first sentence, your **Introduction** is very important. Some people, however, find it difficult to write a good introduction.

The following technique will help you to write good introductions when writing a letter or email.

### I Want To Inform You That...(For Letters Or Emails)

Using the above expression, you can capture the main point that you want to convey. To do so, start your draft letter with the following words, "I want to tell you that...." or "I want to inform you that..."

Here are some examples:

- *I want to inform you that the president will be visiting your office on Friday, December 5th, 20XX.*

- *I want to inform you that the Yatota Ping Pong team won the 21st annual sports competition in Oslo this year.*

- *I want to inform you that you are invited to a party at 451 Sabran Lane, Sussex.*

Once you are sure that the first line captures what you truly want to say, you may cancel the first part, i.e., "I want to tell you that" or "I want to inform you that…"

For example,

> ~~I want to inform you that~~ *The president will be visiting your office on Friday, December 5th, 20xx.*

> ~~I want to inform you that~~ *The Yatota Ping Pong team won the 21st annual sports competition in Oslo this year.*

> ~~I want to inform you that~~ *You are invited to a party at 451 Sabran Lane, Sussex.*

## Short Paragraphs are All Right

Businesspeople are busy people. Get straight to the point at the beginning of your email or letter. You do not have to write long-winded paragraphs and bury the most important thing you want to say.

Short paragraphs make your writing more inviting to read. Note that it is even possible to have a one-line paragraph.

# Assignment 20
**Exercise: I want to tell you that...**

**Using the phrase "I want to tell you that..." as a starting point, try to create a sentence that could serve as an introduction to a letter or email.**

Example: New website design

> \* ~~I want to tell you that~~...Our company's website will be redesigned in the coming weeks.

> \* Our company's website will be redesigned in the coming weeks.

1. Urgent meeting: _____

2. New IT staff member: _____

3. Earthquake drill: _____

4. New food delivery service: _____

5. Year-end party: _____
_____
_____

6. Teleconference meeting: _____
_____
_____

7. Invitation of colleagues to a routine meeting: _____
_____
_____

8. Request to borrow an item from a colleague: _____
_____
_____

9. Inquiry about a negotiation seminar to be held next month: ___
_____
_____

10. A complaint: _____
_____
_____

# Assignment 21
## Form sentences with the verbs below.

1. retrain: _____

_____

2. resolve: _____

_____

3. queue: _____

_____

4. erode: _____

_____

5. reenter: _____

_____

6. pool: _____

_____

7. reclaim: _____

_____

8. recognize: _____

_____

9. reconstruct: _____

_____

10. plot: _____

_____

11. raise: _____

_____

12. realize: _____

_____

13. quicken: _____

_____

14. recall: _____

_____

15. rate: _____

_____

16. provide: _____

_____

17. telecommute: _____

_____

18. televise: _____

_____

19. tabulate: _____

_____

20. submit: _____

_____

21. plant: _____

_____

22. arbitrate: _____

_____

23. outperform: _____

_____

24. outline: _____

_____

25. outrun: _____

_____

26. enlist: _____

_____

27. encompass: _____

_____

28. enthrall: _____

_____

# FUN WITH GRAMMAR #6

**Choose the correct answer from each pair of italicized words or phrases.**

1. Every child **need/needs** attention.

2. The population of India **is/are** over 1 billion.

3. Each of my friends **read/reads** one book a week.

4. One of the most challenging problems today **is/are** global warming.

5. Both boys and girls **is/are** capable of learning complex concepts.

6. Three hours **is/are** too much for making an omelet.

7. A red and yellow rabbit **stand/is standing** on the desk.

8. Almost half of the land **is/are** covered with water.

9. Eating too much chocolate **is/are** bad.

10. A red rabbit and a yellow rabbit **sit/sits** on the chair every day.

# Unit 7
## Common Errors in Business Writing

The same mistakes often come up again and again in business writing. This is good news. It means that if you are able to overcome these errors, you could improve your writing considerably.

Here are a few of them:

- Too many words (save your reader time by getting to the point)
- Use of jargon, technical words, and unfamiliar acronyms (if the reader doesn't understand the word or term, you have not properly shared your message)
- Lack of organization (use an outline/have a plan before you begin)

## Get Editing Help

It is difficult for some writers to check their own work. But every writer ought to make the effort. You may also get someone to check your writing, especially if it is a long report. If it is a short report or letter, sometimes, all you need to do is put it aside for a while and get back to it later. When you return to the work with a pair of fresh eyes you often see things that you could not see before.

## Mind your tone

Often, how we say something is just as important as what we say. Sometimes, long after people have forgotten what we said, they might still remember how what we said affected them. Human beings are creatures of emotion. This includes businesspeople! So, it is important to consider your tone. It is, perhaps, with this in mind that American poet Maya Angelou wrote,

> *I've learned that people will forget what you said, people will forget what you did, but people will never forget how you made them feel.*

If you do not craft your message carefully, it is possible for the reader to feel disrespected or even attacked. Please mind your tone.

## Logical flow

Making use of a brief outline can be very useful. It can be as simple as a point-by-point list of the topics you want to cover. Make sure that the points follow a logical order up to the conclusion. Once you have the points down, think hard about how you can seize the reader's attention.

If you do not grab the reader in the first few seconds, you cannot guarantee that he or she will read on till the end.

## Welcome plain language

For decades, English speakers maintained a somewhat rigid separation between the spoken language and the written language. Written English often involved multisyllabic words and long sentences. Readers sometimes had to go look for their dusty dictionaries to find out what the writer was trying to say. Spoken language, however, has often been more direct. Remember the advice, "Write like you talk?" If you write as though you were talking directly to the reader, you can't go wrong.

## Say no to clichés

Clichés are overused phrases. When such phrases first came into fashion, they may have seemed fresh, but after being used over and over again, they no longer seem fresh. You are better off creating your own fresh-sounding expressions than relying on clichés to carry your writing along.

Here's a sampling of clichés: *ace in the hole; airing dirty laundry; ace up your sleeve; back to square one; acid test; all in a day's work; all hat, no cattle; death and destruction; back against the wall*

# Assignment 22

You have been working with a printing company for the last 18 months, but they are always late with your work and there have been times when their mistakes have delayed your projects. You want to end your company's relationship with them.

Send an email to the Head of Operations, Ms Jana Smithson, explaining your decision.

# Assignment 23

A local newspaper wants to interview you for a feature on business people. They would like to know when their reporter can visit you and where you would like to have the interview done. Reply to Managing Editor, Ms Sheila Langston.

# Assignment 24
**Form sentences with the verbs below.**

1. empower: _____

2. evolve: _____

3. evangelize: _____

4. examine: _____

5. excel: _____

6. campaign: _____

7. adhere: _____

8. absorb: _____

9. acquaint: _____

10. acknowledge: _____

_____

11. account: _____

_____

12. exchange: _____

_____

13. extrapolate: _____

_____

14. exercise: _____

_____

15. film: _____

_____

16. encourage: _____

_____

17. decorate: _____

_____

18. correct: _____

_____

19. sort: _____

_____

# Assignment 25
**Write an email to a friend and share what you've learned from Unit 7.**

# FUN WITH GRAMMAR #7
**Write in the blank space the plural of the word in parentheses.**

1. Two _____ are standing on the roof. *(man)*

2. Human beings have thirty-two _____ . *(tooth)*

3. _____ are easy to prepare. *(sandwich)*

4. _____ should be stored properly. *(knife)*

5. Some people use washing machines to clean _____ . *(potato)*

6. What are the _____ for selecting astronauts? *(criterion)*

7. The school is trying out various _____ . *(curriculum)*

8. _____ are very useful for people who are isolated. *(radio)*

9. In Japan, _____ are required of job applicants. *(photo)*

10. Pharmaceutical researchers find _____ very useful in their work. *(mouse)*

# Unit 8
## The Reader's Need: Revisited

The reader is king, queen, prince, or princess – take your pick.

If you want to write letters that get quick replies and results, keep your reader forever in mind. Don't keep the attention on you; shine the spotlight on the reader.

Keeping your reader in mind means, first of all, using words that the reader will understand. If you are using words and expressions that require the reader to pick up the dictionary every few words, you might lose the attention you seek. If you are using too many "me's" and "I's" — beware. Rather, let "you" (that is, the reader) be the center of attention.

## Analyze the reader

Analyze your reader. Think about your reader's possible needs. If you are aware of the level of knowledge of your client or potential reader, you are more likely to adopt the correct tone and send just the right amount of information that the reader needs. Can you put yourself in the reader's position?

## No benefit of eye contact!

When you send an email, you do not have the benefit of eye contact, gestures, or other face-to-face communication signals with the reader. Your writing, therefore, ought to be able to stand on its own! Make sure that what you have written will hold the reader's attention till the end. Otherwise, the letter, memo, or report will be put aside, and promptly forgotten.

## Call for action

Let the reader know how you want him or her to respond. Do you want the reader to telephone you? Wire funds? Buy your product?

Readers do not have to guess what you want them to do. So, be explicit. Be clear in making the request, though politely.

## Assignment 26
**Form sentences with the verbs below.**

1. eliminate: _____
_____

2. perplex: _____
_____

3. emerge: _____
_____

4. justify: _____
_____

5. engage: _____
_____

6. compose: _____
_____

7. determine: _____
_____

# Assignment 27

Your company has purchased some equipment from a foreign company and wired 6 million yen in payment. Write an email to the company informing them of when you sent the funds and asking for them to confirm receipt as well as tell you when you will receive their products.

## Assignment 28

**Dear Sir/Madam:**

**We are considering using your company's services. Please let us know what makes your company different from your competitors.**

**Sincerely,**
**Rhonda Rowad**

# Assignment 29
## Form sentences with the verbs below.

1. process: _____

2. network: _____

3. legalize: _____

4. laminate: _____

5. co-opt: _____

6. construe: _____

7. compete: _____

8. deregulate: _____

9. digitize: _____

10. elaborate: _____

_____

11. elbow: _____

_____

12. elevate: _____

_____

13. emphasize: _____

_____

14. intuit: _____

_____

15. invent: _____

_____

16. improve: _____

_____

17. normalize: _____

_____

18. legislate: _____

_____

19. deceive: _____

_____

# FUN WITH GRAMMAR #8

**Choose the correct answer from each pair of italicized words.**

1. The chair fell on the ***managers'/manager's*** leg.

2. My ***uncle's/uncles'*** son is my cousin.

3. The company specializes in ***lady's/ladies'*** watches.

4. The ***boss'/bosses'*** wife is an engineer.

5. A ***diplomat's/diplomats'*** work sounds exciting.

6. The ***speaker's/speakers'*** bureau has a list of 100 motivational speakers.

7. ***Children's/Childrens'*** books can be a lot of fun to read.

8. The ***professor's/professors'*** arm got caught in the swing.

9. My ***wife's/wives'*** ball gown looks splendid.

10. ***Akikos/Akiko's*** plan was accepted.

# Unit 9
## Know Your Formats

There are many different kinds of formats for written communication. A memo is not a letter and a fax is not an email. Each has its own special format. Being aware of such formats can help you reach your reader in a medium that is both familiar and appropriate.

## Common Letter Formats:
- Full Block
- Semi-block/Modified Block

There are many formats for letters but the two mentioned above are the most commonly used. Decide on one style and stick with it. It will make your life easier. In some cases, the company you work for may have decided on a style – a preferred house style – so all you have to do is confirm which one it is and stick with it.

# Full Block Style

Ms Johnetta Bigsby[4]　　　　　　　　　　　<==　　{Sender's name}
Write Right International Consultants　　<==　　{Name of sender's company}
17 Lodestar Avenue　　　　　　　　　　　　<==　　{Sender's address}
Port Angeles, WA
98620 USA

Tel: (360) 555-6666　　　　　　　　　　　<==　　{Sender's telephone number}

December 7, 20XX　　　　　　　　　　　　<==　　{Date letter written}

Mr Willy Bakuroyokoyama　　　　　　　　<==　　{Recipient's name}
Bakubaku Shoji Ltd.　　　　　　　　　　<==　　{Name of recipient's company}
7-7-1 Higashi Shinjuku　　　　　　　　　<==　　{Recipient's address}
Shinjuku-ku, Tokyo
150-9876

Dear Mr Willy Bakuroyokoyama:　　　　　　　{Note use of colon in salutation/ comma also OK}

SUBJECT: Full Block

Your desire to choose a house style for your letters is an admirable one.

We highly recommend the Full Block style because it is easy to use. Everything starts from the left, whether it's the recipient's address, date, salutation or complimentary close. Of course, if you are using a letterhead then you do not have to write down the address of the sender (yours), as this would already be shown on the letterhead.

Following the complimentary close, be sure to include your name and leave ample space, about four lines, for your signature. You may also include your title.

Sincerely,


Johnetta Bigsby
Writing Consultant

---

4  Sender's name here may be omitted

# **Modified Block Style**

|  |  |  |
|---|---|---|
| {Sender's name} | ==> | Ms Johnetta Bigsby[5] |
| {Name of sender's company} |  | Write Right International Consultants |
| {Sender's address} |  | 17 Lodestar Avenue |
|  |  | Port Angeles, WA |
|  |  | 98620 USA |
|  |  |  |
| {Sender's telephone number} ==> |  | Tel: (360) 555-6666 |
|  |  |  |
| {Date letter written} | ==> | December 7, 20XX |

| | | |
|---|---|---|
| Mr Willy Bakuroyokoyama | <== | {Recipient's name} |
| Bakubaku Shoji Ltd. | <== | {Name of recipient's company} |
| 7-7-1 Higashi Shinjuku | <== | {Recipient's address} |
| Shinjuku-ku, Tokyo | | |
| 150-9876 | | |

Dear Mr Willy Bakuroyokoyama:    <==    {Note use of colon in salutation/ comma also OK}

SUBJECT: Modified block style

Your desire to choose a house style for your letters is a good idea.

An option you might want to consider is the Modified Block Style. In this case, the sender's name, address, and date, as well as the complimentary close and signature block, are indented towards the right. Everything else stays on the left.

Following the complimentary close, be sure to include your name and leave ample space, about four lines, for your signature. You may also include your title.

    {Complimentary Close}    Sincerely,




                            Johnetta Bigsby
    {Job title}            Writing Consultant

---

[5] Sender's name here may be omitted

## Assignment 30
You have just received an email from an old friend. He writes:

Hey buddy,
What's up? You're doing all right, I hope. I'm kinda struggling in my new job. You see, my boss has been giving me all kinds of writing assignments. I have heard that you are taking a business writing course. Send me some tips ASAP on how I can improve my writing.

Cheers,
Peter Lamkin (Your Old Friend — Still Young!)

# Assignment 31

Ms Zana Lattimer has worked in your office for five years. She is leaving in the next two weeks, both because of family issues and the need to explore new professional horizons abroad. She is an exceptionally good employee and you want to express your sadness at her impending departure and to wish her well in her future endeavors.

# Assignment 32
**Form sentences with the verbs below.**

1. annotate: _____

2. monitor: _____

3. mortgage: _____

4. multiply: _____

5. narrate: _____

6. nurse: _____

7. obtain: _____

8. overwhelm: _____

9. overwork: _____

10. overhear: _____

_____

11. quit: _____

_____

12. proofread: _____

_____

13. protest: _____

_____

14. replenish: _____

_____

15. report: _____

_____

16. update: _____

_____

17. simplify: _____

_____

18. transmit: _____

_____

19. translate: _____

_____

# FUN WITH GRAMMAR #9

**Choose the correct answer from each pair of italicized words.**

1. Every singer **know/knows** the value of good breathing techniques.

2. Cooking **has/have** become popular among businesspeople.

3. Statistics **are/is** my favorite subject.

4. A lot of the equipment on the construction site **are/is** useless.

5. The number of tables needed **are/is** ten.

6. A number of scientists **is/are** working on a cure for cancer.

7. Each player **has/have** a jersey.

8. Each of the marathon runners **deserve/deserves** praise.

9. Most of the children's homework **is/are** badly done.

10. Statistics **is/are** often used to lie to people.

# Unit 10
## Memorandum (Memo)

Remember the following key points about memos:

1) There is usually no complimentary close
   (i.e., Yours faithfully, Yours sincerely, Best regards, etc.)
2) Memos are for internal purposes
3) The purpose is to provide information, request action, or make a recommendation
4) Memos often mention action items (things that must be done)

## Memo types:
- information reports
- problem-solving reports
- persuasive reports
- proposals

### MEMO Format

TO:
FROM:
DATE:
SUBJECT:

_____

_____

_____

_____

# Sample Memo

To:       All Employees
From:     K. Mochizuki                              cc:
Date:     Oct 17, 20XX
Subject:  Earthquake Drill

---

Please be informed that there will be an earthquake drill, as follows:

    Date:  October 31, 20XX
    Time:  7:30 am – 9:30 am
    Place:  Reception area — 17th Floor (Sundance Building)

All employees are required to attend this drill. In case you are not able to attend, please inform Ms Yuki Sakurai, Human Resources, at 03-XXXX-YYYY by Oct 16, 20XX.

# Assignment 33

**A colleague from another country is coming to work with you. She is not sure exactly what your job entails and wants you to send a brief description of what you do.**

# Assignment 34

A senior executive, Ms Shivangi Harper, is going to take over the leadership of your section and wants you to send her an email describing a project you are working on now or one that you worked on in the past.

# Assignment 35
**Form sentences with the verbs below.**

1. tamp: _____

2. succeed: _____

3. strive: _____

4. stroll: _____

5. validate: _____

6. vary: _____

7. voice: _____

8. volunteer: _____

9. truncate: _____

10. undertake: _____

_____

11. terminate: _____

_____

12. toughen: _____

_____

13. transcribe: _____

_____

14. transfer: _____

_____

15. underscore: _____

_____

16. verify: _____

_____

17. revitalize: _____

_____

18. vindicate: _____

_____

19. waive: _____

_____

## Assignment 36

**Mr Kojo Sweeney helped you prepare some PowerPoint slides. Send a brief email of thanks to him. Be sure to mention that you will need his help again in the near future. Also, give him the assurance that you will be taking steps to learn the program so that you do not have to depend on him forever.**

# Assignment 37: USE YOUR THESAURUS

| | Find synonyms for SAY | a. Find the exact meaning of each word using a dictionary<br>b. Use the word in a sentence of your own |
|---|---|---|
| 1 | | a. |
| | | b. |
| 2 | | a. |
| | | b. |
| 3 | | a. |
| | | b. |
| 4 | | a. |
| | | b. |
| 5 | | a. |
| | | b. |

# FUN WITH GRAMMAR #10
**Correct the errors.**

1. It is obviously a computer's error.

2. Airplanes pilots must be able to react quickly.

3. Computers's skills are becoming more and more important.

4. I took a three-hours examination last Friday.

5. Lily has a seven-years-old brother.

6. Dr Finkelstein is a university's professor.

7. Dr Kimiko Ogawa is a teachers teacher.

8. A five-hours flight is not so bad.

9. I have fifteen years' experience as an editor.

10. Taxis drivers in London apparently have bigger brains!

# Unit 11
## Writing Frameworks

Writing frameworks are useful for those days when you are pressed for time and you need to write something quickly. A framework gives you a preorganized way to structure your ideas.

Here are some examples:

## 1. PPF – Past, Present, Future

Let's say your topic is: My work experience

Using PPF you might say something like this:

> In the past, that is, when I was in university, I worked part-time as a youth coordinator. In this job, I was responsible for providing advice to a group of young people who had dropped out of school but were thinking of going back. I had to do a lot of research to find the right information for the students. In fact, even though I was supposed to help the students, I ended up benefiting most of all because I learned a great deal about how to do research and find reliable sources.
>
> At present, I am a stock trader. It is a high-pressure job but I love it because it gives me an opportunity to work with analysts and to interview company leaders. Even though I am still relatively young, I get to interact with a lot of experienced people and many of them are generous with advice. I think that all the advice I am receiving will help me in my career over time.
>
> In the future, I would like to go back to school and get another degree. My goal is to teach in the university, possibly in the field of business. I may be able to combine theory with practical business knowledge to help students who aspire to enter the business world. For now, I want to do as well as I can in anything I tackle, but I do not think I will be ready for any kind of major change until after four or five years.

## 2. PREP
P - Point
R - Reason
E - Example
P - Point

The PREP framework can be considered a basic paragraph.

Let's say your topic is something as simple as fine dining in Tokyo.

Using PREP, you first make a point, for example, "Tokyo is a mecca for fine dining, and then follow it up with a reason."

P:  Tokyo is a mecca for fine dining.
R:  ...because Tokyo even beats Paris when it comes to the number of Michelin-starred restaurants in the city.
E:  For instance, it is possible to get a wide range of fine food, including French, Italian, and Thai in Tokyo. Some of these restaurants are charming little places — hidden gems, really.
P:  If you are a food lover, as I am, Tokyo is where you need to be to eat your way around the world.

## 3. The Twist – The Change – The Shift
People change; businesses change; societies change. There are times when you may have to write about such a change in your business, your department, or your life. In such a case, you can write about how things used to be, then mention something that happened to trigger a change (new management, a shocking event, change of policy, etc.), and then go on to the kinds of changes that were made and how successful, or not, those changes may have been.

# Assignment 38

Write about change in some aspect of your business — marketing, products, or service.

**Think about:**  a) The way things were before
b) What triggered the change
c) The effect of the change

# Assignment 39

You have just mailed a package of your company's services to Ms Lanelle Fox. It will take two days to arrive.

Send her an email to let her know about the package you sent. Also, give her your contact information in case she has any questions that she needs answered.

# Assignment 40
## Form sentences with the verbs below.

1. weigh: _____

2. wean: _____

3. wholesale: _____

4. withdraw: _____

5. verbalize: _____

6. venerate: _____

7. videotape: _____

8. utilize: _____

9. retrieve: _____

10. return: _____

_____

11. sail: _____

_____

12. rush: _____

_____

13. route: _____

_____

14. rotate: _____

_____

15. revise: _____

_____

16. solicit: _____

_____

17. solve: _____

_____

18. spike: _____

_____

19. specify: _____

_____

# Assignment 41

A customer was put on hold for twenty minutes and forgotten. She has threatened to stop doing business with your company. Write an apology letter to her. She is Ms Yvette Fernando.

# FUN WITH GRAMMAR #11

**Choose the correct answer from each pair of italicized words or phrases.**

1. Mrs Bella Balala is **competent/a competent** manager.

2. Mr Kinjo is delighted **to/with** his new position.

3. She was delighted **to/with** meet me.

4. The caterer **apologies/apologized** for the mixup.

5. Lennox enjoys **to read/reading** business books.

6. The head office is **apposite/opposite** the theatre.

7. Ms Pinto **quite/quiet** likes her job.

8. **While/During** the technician was speaking, someone took a picture.

9. There was no **evidences/evidence** that the company had committed any crime.

10. She **must of/must have** completed her preparations for the summer.

# Unit 12
## The Paragraph

In your career, you may not only have to write emails and letters; you may have to write reports. When you have to write a report or an article, you realize how important paragraphs are. If you can write paragraphs that are logical and coherent, you have a headstart.

### Opening With A Topic Sentence

The very first sentence of a paragraph can be used to make an important point. This is called the *topic sentence.*

You probably remember PREP: Point, Reason, Example, Point.

That framework, PREP, is a simple one for creating a paragraph. Of course, depending on the topic you are writing on, this can expand a bit more so that instead of providing one reason and one example, you might provide a couple of reasons and several examples. But, at the most basic level, you **make a point** at the beginning. It is then followed by a **reason**, an **example** or two, and a final **point** that wraps up everything in that paragraph. This final point reinforces the first one in the reader's mind. It is also a signal that you have finished and that you are ready to move on to the next idea.

Consider someone's thoughts on the city of Tokyo:

> *<u>Tokyo is a wonderful city.</u> It has all the amenities one might expect in a city and more. It is the kind of place that both children and adults love. You can play all day at arcades and dance all night in clubs if you put your mind to it. I think Tokyo is one of the best places in the world.*

# Assignment 42
**For your company's newsletter editor, write a brief piece about**
**a) a *company* milestone that impressed you...or**
**b) an interesting company event you attended**

# Assignment 43
## Form sentences with the verbs below.

1. set up: _____

_____

2. sanitize: _____

_____

3. sponsor: _____

_____

4. save: _____

_____

5. sew: _____

_____

6. spread: _____

_____

7. unite: _____

_____

8. trust: _____

_____

9. trace: _____

_____

10. thwart: _____

11. trade: _____

12. subcontract: _____

13. surf: _____

14. survey: _____

15. support: _____

16. survive: _____

17. syndicate: _____

18. synthesize: _____

19. supply: _____

## Assignment 44

**Your company's newsletter editor wants you to write a brief article about an important *personal* milestone in your life. Please make sure that there is an introduction, body, and conclusion.**

# Assignment 45

**Your supervisor says:** "We need a new fax machine. Send an email to KokuFax Incorporated (info@kokufax.jp) and ask them to send us a copy of their latest catalog. Also, find out if they can send a salesperson to our office some time next week."

# Assignment 46

| Prepositional Phrases | Form a Sentence with each of the Listed Prepositional Phrases |
|---|---|
| Care for | |
| Be cluttered with | |
| Be committed to | |
| Compare to | |
| Compare with | |
| Complain about | |
| Complain of | |
| Be composed of | |

# FUN WITH GRAMMAR #12
## Count and noncount nouns

1. Some of the clothing in the bag *is/are* good.

2. Mathematics *is/are* as much fun as grammar.

3. Very few schools use *chalk/chalks* today.

4. The evidence *are/is* insufficient.

5. Laughter *is/are* the language of love.

6. American *slangs/slang* is fun to listen to.

7. Most babies have no *hair/hairs.*

8. Intelligence *is/are* not only about solving problems on paper.

9. I got a lot of *advice/advices* from friends.

10. Patience *are/is* often necessary for patients.

# Unit 13
## Sentence Variation

It is said that variety is the soul of pleasure. This is certainly true of the scenery you observe as you take a slow train ride across the countryside.

When it comes to writing as well, variety is important. The same sentence structure might be fun to write for a while but the reader soon gets tired of it. Varying the length of your sentences and the patterns of your sentences can make your writing less boring.

### You Don't Need a Sentence One Kilometer Long

Some writers are famous for writing long sentences. By the time you come to the end of such a sentence, you have practically forgotten what it was supposed to be about. Please don't write such long sentences.

Let's start with the simplest of sentences and build up to longer ones.

A sentence can be as simple as any of the following:

> *The sun rises.*
> *I think of fruit flies everyday.*

## The Simple Sentence

A simple sentence has these key ingredients: a subject and a verb and carries meaning.

| **Subject** | **Verb** | |
|---|---|---|
| Vivian | likes | mangoes. |
| The teacher | loves | Shakespeare. |
| Students | review | for their exams. |
| The soccer player | heads | the ball. |

## Clause

A clause, according to www.learnersdictionary.com, is "a part of a sentence that has its own subject and verb."

## Independent Clauses

The above sentences can stand on their own. As such, they are INDEPENDENT.

## Compound and Complex Sentences

Beyond the simple sentence, we will learn about compound and complex sentences. For now, let's review another type of clause.

## Dependent Clauses

While the independent clause can stand on its own, dependent clauses are like infants. They cannot stand on their own; they need to combine with an independent clause.

Look at the following: *As soon as I get the money...*

The above clause cannot stand on its own. It is a dependent clause. It needs another family of words, an independent clause, to help it to become complete.

*As soon as I get the money, I shall go to Timbuktu.*

Let's break the sentence into two and examine each part.

> *As soon as I get the money,...*    <== *Dependent clause*
> *I shall go to Timbuktu.*    <== *Independent clause*

When the two parts, the dependent clause and the independent clause are put together, they make sense. An independent clause can make sense on its own but a dependent clause needs an independent clause to make sense. Dependent clauses are usually linked to subordinating conjunctions such as the following:

| SUBORDINATING CONJUNCTIONS ||
|---|---|
| after | once |
| although | provided |
| as | provided that |
| as far as | rather than |
| as if | since |
| as long as | so that |
| as much as | supposing |
| as soon as | that |
| as though | though |
| because | till |
| before | unless |
| even | until |
| even if | when |
| even though | whenever |
| if | where |
| if only | whereas |
| if when | where if |
| if then | wherever |
| inasmuch | whether |
| in order that | which |
| just as | while |
| lest | who |
| now | whoever |
| now that | why |

Consider the following:

*As far as I am concerned,...*

The expression, "*As far as I am concerned,...*" is an example of a dependent clause. It cannot stand on its own.

*As far as I am concerned, Jonathan is a good guy.*
    {dependent clause}    {main clause}

The dependent clause cannot stand on its own. The main (independent) clause can stand on its own.

# Assignment 47
## Which part of the following is dependent and which independent?

1. Whenever I am sad, I write in my journal.
    {          }{          }

2. When spring comes, all flowers bloom.
    {          } {          }

3. Even if you fail, you should not give up.
    {          }{          }

4. They get excited when their favorite team comes to town.
    {          }{          }

5. I write in my journal whenever I am feeling excited.
    {          }{          }

## Recap: subordinate clauses

Words and phrases such as "even though," "although," and "in order that" are called subordinating conjunctions. When these subordinating conjunctions are attached to a phrase, that expression cannot stand on its own.

Learning to write sentences that combine dependent clauses and independent clauses allows you to express a wider range of meaning.

## Compound Sentences

A compound sentence has two or more independent clauses but no dependent clauses.

> The boss invited the workers to lunch, and she paid the tab.

Each of the underlined group of words above is an independent clause. Each can stand on its own; each makes sense. In a compound sentence, the two parts are joined by coordinating conjunctions such as ***for, and, nor, but, or, yet, so.***

Coordinating conjunctions connect two clauses that have roughly equal standing or weight. Here's a way for you to remember these coordinating conjunctions:

| F | A | N | B | O | Y | S |
|---|---|---|---|---|---|---|
| for | and | nor | but | or | yet | so |

You can also use a semicolon to join two independent clauses. For example,
*Punctuality is important; my company does not tolerate lateness.*

# Assignment 48

**Write five compound sentences, one each on the subjects below. Note that a compound sentence is one that has at least two independent clauses. (FANBOYS may help you out!)**

1. conference: _____

_____

_____

2. experience: _____

_____

_____

3. mistake: _____

_____

_____

4. investment: _____

_____

_____

5. surprise: _____

_____

_____

## Complex Sentences

A complex sentence has one independent clause and at least one dependent clause. A dependent clause cannot stand on its own even though it has a subject and a verb. The dependent clause, however, can combine with an INDEPENDENT clause.

For example,

He called a meeting after sending out the mail.
   INDEPENDENT         DEPENDENT

After the cashier tallied up her sales, she discovered she was short by 3,000 yen.
   DEPENDENT                              INDEPENDENT

## Assignment 49
**Write five complex sentences on the subjects below.**

1. coffee shops: _____

_____

_____

2. hiring: _____

_____

_____

3. skyscrapers: _____

_____

_____

4. foreign exchange: _____

_____

_____

5. competition: _____

_____

_____

## Complex-Compound Sentences

A complex-compound sentence has **two or more** independent clauses and at least one dependent clause.

A business leader needs to have a vision, and because business throws up so many challenges, a business leader needs to have a reliable team around her.

Independent clauses:
> *A business leader needs to have a vision.*
> *A business leader needs to have a reliable team around her.*

Dependent clause:
> *..... because business throws up so many challenges,*

# Assignment 50
**Write five complex-compound sentences on the subjects below.**

1. hotels: _____

_____

_____

2. stock market: _____

_____

_____

3. bonus: _____

_____

_____

4. decisions: _____

_____

_____

5. waste: _____

_____

_____

Having a mix of sentence patterns in your writing is a more mature way of writing letters, emails, and reports. You can also read your sentences aloud to ensure that you have rhythm and flow. Good writing is like good music. It flows well; it is not choppy.

# Assignment 51
**Combine the following into compound, complex, or compound-complex sentences.**

1. We did our work quickly. We rushed to the meeting room. There was no meeting going on.

2. JR Tokai and High Speed Rail. They operate bullet trains in Taiwan. They will sign a contract within a few months. They will combine to lay a new railway line.

3. Rakuten President Hiroshi Mikitani wants the government to set clear tax targets. Rakuten President Hiroshi Mikitani wants the government to set clear employment targets. This will strengthen the country's international competitiveness.

4. Libraries are successfully moving from analog to the digital age. They provide access to a wide range of digital and multimedia tools. These tools will prepare future generations with 21st century technology skills.

_____

_____

_____

_____

## Cardinal Numbers and Dates

When you are writing dates, use cardinal numbers (1, 2, 3, 4, 5, 6, 7, 8, etc.) rather than ordinal numbers (1st, 2nd, 3rd, 4th, 5th, 6th, 7th, 8th, etc.).

For example,

> *We shall hold the workshop on November 16, 20XX.*

> *On February 8, 20XX, we shall hold an orientation session for new employees.*

## Assignment 52

You had been negotiating with a company, Bambers Trust, over the last five months to sell them some products. You've come to an agreement on both price and terms. This morning, you got an email from the head of the company asking for 5% more reduction on the price you had agreed upon. You really want to do business with this company. At the same time, a 5% reduction will hurt your business badly. Send an email to Ms Zellenika Omamu, CEO, of Bambers Trust.

# FUN WITH GRAMMAR #13

**Choose the correct answer from each pair of italicized words.**

1. The design was ***especial/especially*** clever.

2. Putting all your cards on the table in a negotiation puts you at a ***disadvantage/unadvantage.***

3. It is not ***advisible/advisable*** to work for several days without sleep.

4. The vendor was very ***apologizing/apologetic*** after delivering the wrong products.

5. It is always a challenge to ***chose/choose*** among several excellent candidates.

6. It is ***unwise/nonwiserly*** to make a habit of fighting with everyone at the office.

7. Some companies exist for the ***sole/soul*** purpose of imitating others.

8. Businesses should be aware of both opportunities and ***treats/threats.***

9. Every company should take an interest in the professional ***grow/growth*** of its employees.

10. How a company ***differences/differentiates*** itself from others is critical.

# Unit 14
## Getting Comfortable with Writing

For some people, the problem with writing is that it is difficult to put anything down on paper. Being a good writer is as much a matter of skill as of habit. This is why freewriting is recommended to train mind and muscles to work together. After all, a person who has to write on the job cannot rely solely on inspiration. When a report is needed and you are the one responsible for it, your excuses can only go so far. Pretty soon, you have to sit down and write.

## Freewriting

With freewriting, your goal is just to become comfortable with the idea of writing regularly. Your goal is not necessarily to produce a masterpiece. Once you get used to the idea of writing often, however, who knows what gems you might produce? When you are doing a freewriting exercise, try to write on and on and on. You might try to focus on a theme and develop it, but if the writing sends you in another direction, do not resist it. Keep going. Even when you think you are stuck, you can keep going by writing about the difficulty you are facing at that moment. Thus, freewriting is an exercise that lets you burn your bridges, leaving you with no excuse for retreat.

**Sample** *This is supposed to be a freewriting exercise but, but, but, oh my God, writing is so difficult. Why is it that some people find it so easy but I find it so hard? I am able to talk freely with my friends and even total strangers, but when it comes to writing, I am at a complete loss. I will pay a billion bucks to anyone who can help me out of this problem. And speaking of problem, I am.....*

# Assignment 53
**Freewriting: Ready, Set, Go!**

# Brainstorming

Brainstorming is useful for generating ideas; the main point is to open the floor so that anyone can share his or her idea freely on a given subject.

These ideas may be written down on a board or jotted down on a piece of paper. One key element of brainstorming is that during the idea-generating phase, no one is allowed to criticize the suggestions made.

The goal is to write down as many ideas as possible and to select from among these those that seem promising. Some writing projects could use brainstorming as a starting point in order to ensure that everything that is important is covered.

While brainstorming is associated with groups, nothing prevents you from doing your own private brainstorming to generate ideas for a writing project.

# 5 Ws & 1 H
**Who, What, When, Where, Why and How**

The above question words have been used by journalists for years. Children also use them to good effect. Use these to help you consider what kinds of questions the reader might want answered.

# Assignment 54
## Form sentences with the verbs below.

1. transport: _____
_____

2. troubleshoot: _____
_____

3. truck: _____
_____

4. strengthen: _____
_____

5. structure: _____
_____

6. submit: _____
_____

7. summarize: _____
_____

8. supervise: _____
_____

9. toil: _____
_____

10. track: _____

_____

11. staff: _____

_____

12. streamline: _____

_____

13. sterilize: _____

_____

14. stimulate: _____

_____

15. subsidize: _____

_____

16. standardize: _____

_____

17. anticipate: _____

_____

18. analyze: _____

_____

19. assert: _____

_____

## Assignment 55

**You have been invited by a client, Ms Melanie Biluyu, to attend a party. You have an important task to complete at work, so you cannot attend. Send Ms Biluyu a brief message explaining that you cannot attend this time.**

# Assignment 56

| Prepositional Phrases | Form a Sentence with each of the Listed Prepositional Phrases |
|---|---|
| Be connected to | |
| Consist of | |
| Be content with | |
| Contribute to | |
| Be convinced of | |
| Be coordinated with | |
| Count on | |
| Be covered with | |

# Assignment 57

You have received a questionnaire from A2Z Seminars and Ms Samantha Soulie, the director, wants to know what the training needs of your employees are. You need to interview all your colleagues to gather information for Ms Soulie. Unfortunately, many employees are on holiday and you will not be able to send the information Ms Soulie wants by her preferred deadline (the end of this week). Send an email to Ms Soulie informing her of the delay.

## Assignment 58: USE YOUR THESAURUS

| | Find synonyms for INQUIRE | a. Find the exact meaning using a dictionary<br>b. Make a sentence |
|---|---|---|
| 1 | | a. |
| | | b. |
| 2 | | a. |
| | | b. |
| 3 | | a. |
| | | b. |
| 4 | | a. |
| | | b. |

# Assignment 59

You have received two books from Can-o-can-aya Books (Fun Family Holidays and Beating Business Blues) and an invoice for ¥37,500. You do not remember ordering any such books. Send an email to orders@can-o-can-aya.jp telling them about the problem. You plan to return the books ASAP and you have decided not to pay for them.

# Assignment 60

## Form sentences with the given verbs.

1. scale: _____

_____

2. oversee: _____

_____

3. orchestrate: _____

_____

4. produce: _____

_____

5. chair: _____

_____

6. control: _____

_____

7. execute: _____

_____

8. organize: _____

_____

9. operate: _____

_____

10. head:_____
_____

11. plan:_____
_____

12. coordinate:_____
_____

13. build:_____
_____

14. administer:_____
_____

15. create:_____
_____

16. accelerate:_____
_____

17. program:_____
_____

18. address:_____
_____

19. apply:_____
_____

20. brief:

21. assemble:

22. authorize:

23. exonerate:

24. vote:

25. stretch:

26. gauge:

27. exhibit:

28. prolong:

# FUN WITH GRAMMAR #14
**Choose the correct answer from each pair of italicized words.**

1. We bought some ***furniture/furnitures*** for the room.

2. The ***scenery/scenerios*** from that mountain road is incredible.

3. The teacher gave us a lot of ***homework/homeworks.***

4. The kid has a large ***vocabulary/vocabularie.***

5. There is too much ***information/informations*** today.

6. We need to get new ***machinery/machineries.***

7. Oranges ***is/are*** great for making drinks.

8. We should reduce the amount of ***garbage/garbages*** in landfills.

9. Studying ***is/are*** a lot of fun.

10. Beauty ***is/are*** almost always welcome anywhere.

11) There ***is/are*** many people in the conference room.

# Unit 15
## Relevance

We always have to make choices when we are writing letters, emails, or reports. If we had all the time in the world, we could write endlessly. But how much information do we really need to share? If a brief letter can get you what you need, why write a long letter and waste both your time and the reader's?

On the other hand, if you need to give background information on a subject and you fail to do so, the recipient might write and ask for clarification. That also wastes time. So, consider carefully how much information you need to convey — not too little and certainly not more than is necessary.

Also, as a businessperson, there are times when, for tactical reasons, you do not want to share certain pieces of information with people who are not entitled to such information. Every company has its secrets, including costs, methods, procedures, or internal relationships. Be discreet.

# Assignment 61

You have been selected to attend a short leadership program at Vanguard University. There are four programs: Advanced Management Program, General Management Program, Program for Leadership Development, and High Potential Leadership Program.

Contact the program coordinator (Ms Shirlee Ronson) and find out all relevant information to help you decide on which course to pursue.

# Assignment 62

A number of companies, including yours, are thinking of moving into a new market. Your boss has asked you to write a brief report about the advantages and disadvantages of being the first mover and of being the second mover. (Do some research if necessary)

# Assignment 63: USE YOUR THESAURUS

| | Find synonyms for SEND | a. Find the exact meaning using a dictionary<br>b. Make a sentence |
|---|---|---|
| 1 | | a.<br><br>b. |
| 2 | | a.<br><br>b. |
| 3 | | a.<br><br>b. |
| 4 | | a.<br><br>b. |

# Assignment 64
## Form sentences with the verbs below.

1. awaken: _____

_____

2. contravene: _____

_____

3. counterbalance: _____

_____

4. deplore: _____

_____

5. discard: _____

_____

6. dismiss: _____

_____

7. dissuade: _____

_____

8. distort: _____

_____

9. economize: _____

_____

10. eject: _____

_____

11. emerge: _____

_____

12. entail: _____

_____

13. extricate: _____

_____

14. devise: _____

_____

15. forfeit: _____

_____

16. generate: _____

_____

17. generalize: _____

_____

18. impede: _____

_____

19. imply: _____

_____

# Assignment 65
## Freewriting: Ready, Set, Go!

# FUN WITH GRAMMAR #15
**Choose the correct answer from each pair of italicized words.**

1. Our delay made the customers very **anger/angry**.

2. Some people draw **strong/strength** from failure.

3. Scientists are saying that **intelligent/intelligence** is important, but so is emotional stability.

4. It is **misery/miserable** when you go camping and it rains nonstop.

5. The **easy/ease** with which she untied the knot left everyone stunned.

6. Being **happiness/happy** is a choice.

7. There is nothing wrong with being a little **adventurious/adventurous**.

8. Being too **caution/cautious** can be costly in business.

9. If you are **determination/determined** enough, you can achieve almost anything.

10. It is always **excited/exciting** to win a prize.

# Unit 16
## The Two-Handed Mouth

The world of business presents many occasions when we have to talk about two sides of an issue: the advantages and disadvantages of investing in a new business or the pros and cons of bringing in an outsider to manage one's employees.

The Two-handed Mouth is just a catchy phrase to remind you to frequently consider two or more sides of an issue.

Now, let's say, you're comparing two companies: Company **A** and Company **B**. You decide to discuss the following three aspects:

> **1**. Company founder
> **2**. Products/Services
> **3**. Leadership

Here's one approach:

> **Introduction**
> Focus on A1
> Focus on B1
>
> Focus on A2
> Focus on B2
>
> Focus on A3
> Focus on B3
> **Conclusion**

Another way is to say all you want about one subject and then go on to say all you want to say about the other.

That would look something like the following:

**Introduction**
Focus on    A1
              A2
              A3

Focus on    B1
              B2
              B3
**Conclusion**

The opportunities for comparison in the world of business are numerous. Here are a few examples:
- pricing plans
- locations
- effectiveness of two approaches
- quality of different products
- seminars/workshops/training methods
- evaluation of presentations

When making comparisons, in addition to showing similarity, you may show differences — contrasts.

# Transition Expressions

When comparing or contrasting, the following transition expressions can be useful:

# Addition

| Expressions for making an additional point ||
|---|---|
| Again | Moreover |
| Also | Even more |
| And | Last |
| Besides | Finally |
| First | Next |
| Further | Secondly |
| Furthermore | Another point is... |
| In addition | In the first place... In the second place |

# Assignment 66

**Choose 10 of the above words or phrases that you seldom use. Form a sentence with each.**

1. _____

2. _____

3. _____

4. _____

5. _____

6. _____

7. _____

8. _____

9. _____

10. _____

## More on Numbers

- When you begin a sentence with a number, spell it out.
    *Fifteen software engineers came to the hackathon.*

- Spell out numbers between 1 and 9.
    *We brought three secretaries along.*
    *We had to reserve five conference rooms.*

- When you write numbers 10 and above, use figures.
    *We had as many as 30 boats in the regatta.*

- Numbers that have technical significance should be kept as figures.
    *Only 5 percent of the land has been cultivated.*

- Numbers that apply to the same thing should be kept consistent.
    *We had 8 people in the first room and 17 people in the second room.*

# Time words and expressions

| Expressions for signaling time ||
|---|---|
| While | Later |
| After | Earlier |
| When | Soon |
| Meanwhile | Sometimes |
| During | Afterwards |
| Next | Following |
| Then | At length |
| So far | This time |
| Immediately | Never |
| Always | Whenever |
| In the meantime | Until now |
| Now | Once |
| Simultaneously | Subsequently |

# Assignment 67

**Choose nine of the above words or phrases that you seldom use. Make a sentence with each.**

1. _____

2. _____

3. _____

4. _____

5. _____

6. _____

7. _____

8. _____

9. _____

## Place words and expressions

| Expressions for signaling place | |
|---|---|
| Here | Nearby |
| Beyond | Neighboring on |
| Adjacent to | Above |
| There | Below |
| Wherever | Kitty-corner from |

## Assignment 68
Make 10 sentences using each of the place words or phrases above.

1. _____

2. _____

3. _____

   _____

4. _____

   _____

5. _____

   _____

6. _____

   _____

7. _____

   _____

8. _____

   _____

9. _____

   _____

10. _____

    _____

# Illustrating a point

| To illustrate  | In particular |
|----------------|---------------|
| For instance   | As an illustration |
| For example    | Specifically |
| To demonstrate | Let me give you an example... |

# Assignment 69
### Use each of the above in a sentence.

1. _____

2. _____

3. _____

4. _____

5. _____

6. _____

7. _____

8. _____

## Comparison

| in the same way  | similarly          |
|------------------|--------------------|
| in like manner   | in similar fashion |
| by the same token| as with A...B....  |
| likewise         | just as A...B...   |

## Assignment 70
### Use each of the above in a sentence.

1. _____

2. _____

3. _____

4. _____

5. _____

6. _____

7. _____

8. _____

## Contrast

| yet | nevertheless |
|---|---|
| nonetheless | while A...B... |
| however | but |
| on the contrary | otherwise |
| on the one hand / on the other hand | notwithstanding |
| and yet | though A...B... |
| after all | even though A...B |
| in contrast | at the same time |

## Assignment 71
**Choose 10 of the above words or phrases that you seldom use and form a sentence with each.**

1. _____

2. _____

3. _____

4. _____

5. _____

6. _____

7. _____

8. _____

9. _____

10. _____

## Cause, Effect, Purpose

| Words and phrases to signal... | | |
|---|---|---|
| **Cause** | **Effect** | **Purpose** |
| because | therefore | in order that |
| since | thus | for this purpose |
| on account of | consequently | so that |
| for that reason | hence | to that end |
|  | accordingly | to this end |
|  | as a result |  |

## Assignment 72

Choose 10 of the above words or phrases that you seldom use and form a sentence with each.

1. _____

2. _____

3. _____

_____

4. _____

_____

5. _____

_____

6. _____

_____

7. _____

_____

8. _____

_____

9. _____

_____

10. _____

_____

## Qualification

| perhaps | always | probably   | although | almost |
|---------|--------|------------|----------|--------|
| nearly  | maybe  | frequently | never    |        |

## Assignment 73
**Choose eight of the above words and use each to form a sentence.**

1. _____

2. _____

3. _____

4. _____

5. _____

6. _____

7. _____

8. _____

# Intensification

| indeed        | to repeat   | by all means   |
| ------------- | ----------- | -------------- |
| of course     | doubtfully  | certainly      |
| without doubt | yes / no    | undoubtedly   |
| in fact       | surely      | most certainly |

# Assignment 74
Choose 10 of the above words or phrases that you seldom use and form a sentence with each.

1. _____

2. _____

3. _____

4. _____

5. _____

6. _____

7. _____

8. _____

9. _____

10. _____

## Clarification

| that is to say | to clarify |
|---|---|
| that is | to explain |
| to put it another way | to rephrase it |
| in other words | to paraphrase |

## Assignment 75
**Use each of the above phrases to form a sentence.**

1. _____

2. _____

3. _____

4. _____

5. _____

6. _____

_____

7. _____

_____

8. _____

_____

## Concession, Summary, and Conclusion

| Concession | Summary | Conclusion |
|---|---|---|
| to be sure | to summarize | in conclusion |
| granted | to sum up | to conclude |
| of course | in sum | finally |
| it is true | in short | lastly |
| even so | in brief | overall |
| nonetheless | in summary | altogether |

## Assignment 76
**Choose 10 of the above words or phrases that you seldom use and form a sentence with each.**

1. _____

_____

2. _____

_____

3. _____

_____

4. _____
_____

5. _____
_____

6. _____
_____

7. _____
_____

8. _____
_____

9. _____
_____

10. _____
_____

# Assignment 77
**What do you like about the city in which you live; what don't you like about it?**

# Assignment 78: Word Watch

**Form a sentence for each of the words and phrase below.**

| WORDS | Form sentences below |
|---|---|
| Effect (noun) | |
| Effect (verb) | |
| Affect (verb) | |
| Already | |
| All ready | |
| Wonder | |
| Wander | |
| Beside | |
| Besides | |

# Assignment 79
**What impressions do you suppose people have of your industry? Please present at least two sides.**

# Assignment 80
## Make sentences with the following verbs.

1. accomplish: _____

_____

2. calculate: _____

_____

3. adapt: _____

_____

4. achieve: _____

_____

5. acquire: _____

_____

6. advance: _____

_____

7. advise: _____

_____

8. advocate: _____

_____

9. arbitrate: _____

_____

10. appoint: _____

_____

11. analyze: _____

_____

12. arrange: _____

_____

13. ascertain: _____

_____

14. assess: _____

_____

15. assist: _____

_____

16. budget: _____

_____

17. chart: _____

_____

18. implement: _____

_____

19. develop: _____

_____

# Assignment 81

**Describe your dream job. How does it differ from your current job? Make sure you have an introduction, body, and conclusion.**

# FUN WITH GRAMMAR #16
## Choose the correct answer from the pair of italicized words.

1. It is **encouraging/encourageous** to see so many young people striving to achieve their goals.

2. There are some **gorgeous/gorgious** artworks in the Tokyo National Museum.

3. Being **nervous/nervatious** before a speech is quite normal.

4. An office that is **sportless/spotless** gives a good impression to clients.

5. Deliberately manipulating others is **repulsive/repolsive**.

6. You will get a **puzzled/puzzleing** look when you ask difficult questions.

7. Many people get **upsized/upset** when they get criticized.

8. The company president bellowed: "I am **pride/proud** of you all."

9. It is **outragible/outrageous** for people to throw litter on the street.

10. The speaker put her notes on the **lectern/lectile** and began her speech.

# Unit 17
## From IDAC to GIDAC

Using IDAC, you can write emails that are straight to the point and businesslike. If all of your emails are like that, however, some of the people you deal with might feel that you lack warmth. After you have been in contact with someone for a while, it is only natural that you show that the relationship has evolved. In this regard, you have to pay close attention to cues from the other person. Some people do not want to be too friendly with their business associates or colleagues. Others expect that after you've got to know them a little better, you will be somewhat friendly towards them. Here's an example of a letter that opens with a greeting.

Dear Jay,

| | |
|---|---|
| **Greeting** | Hope you are having a great day. |
| **Introduction** | I have located the report on medical waste that you requested last week. |
| **Details** | We do not have a soft copy of the text so I am going to scan the pages and send them to you later on today. |
| **Action** | Meanwhile, if you have any other request, please let me know as soon as possible. |
| **Closing** | I look forward to chatting with you shortly. |

Sincerely,
Saleem Bubakar
Senior Engineer

## Think Carefully About Your Greeting

In order to get the greeting right, think about who you are writing to.

Do you already have a business relationship with this person? What is the person's rank? Is it alright to open with a casual greeting? Or would a greeting that is a little more formal be preferable? Don't write long, rambling greetings. Keep your greetings short but warm.

## Assignment 82
### Use each of the following words to form a sentence.

1. adhere (verb) _____

2. aloof (adjective) _____

3. ambiguous (adjective) _____

4. anecdote (noun) _____

5. antagonize (verb) _____

## Assignment 83

**You are going to attend a departmental meeting next week. The chairperson, Ms Junko Haruna, has asked you and others to email suggestions on possible cost cutting in your department. Send your suggestions ASAP to her at: junko.haruna@company.com.**

# Assignment 84

Several of your company's customers have been complaining that their concerns are not resolved quickly enough. As a team leader, write to members of your team suggesting ways for the team to be more responsive to the needs of customers.

## Assignment 85

Your colleague from the accounting department, Ms Selena Yanase, has invited you and others to go for drinks at Architects Café. You have a lot of work to do and might not be able to attend. Reply.

## Assignment 86

**Your colleague from another branch of your company will be visiting the town or city in which you live and wants you to suggest a few must-see places. Reply.**

# Assignment 87

You are going on a business trip. Ms Linda Gustano, the secretary, has booked the KitaYogo Hotel for you. You stayed at this hotel before; it was filthy and not a place you care to spend another night. Send an email to Ms Gustano asking that she find another place for you.

# Assignment 88
## Form sentences with the verbs below.

1. intercede: _____

_____

2. formulate: _____

_____

3. initiate: _____

_____

4. introduce: _____

_____

5. accelerate: _____

_____

6. yield: _____

_____

7. reconcile: _____

_____

8. pioneer: _____

_____

9. deduct: _____

_____

10. diagnose: _____

11. conserve: _____

12. detect: _____

13. convene: _____

14. tolerate: _____

15. dissolve: _____

16. clarify: _____

17. copyright: _____

18. decorate: _____

19. concede: _____

# FUN WITH GRAMMAR #17

**Choose the correct answer from the pair of italicized words or phrases.**

1. The CEO asked us what was **on stake/at stake.**

2. We were asked to provide a **ballpark finger/ballpark figure.**

3. After the meeting, the chairperson said: ***"Let's core it a day!"/"Let's call it a day!"***

4. We realized shortly after the launch that we had made a mistake and that we needed to **cut our losses/catch our losses.**

5. When it comes to ethics, there are so many **gray areas/gray aerials.**

6. Many supervisors want to be kept **in the rope/in the loop** about what is going on in the company.

7. When a relationship just doesn't work it is best to **severe/sever** ties.

8. The new recruit managed to talk the manager **out of/out on** implementing the sales campaign.

9. Whether we will open a new branch in China is all **up in the air/up on the air.**

10. The best form of advertising is said to be **word on mouth/word of mouth.**

# Unit 18
## Good News and Bad News Letters

Businesses send out many routine letters: asking about another company's services, for example. In such cases, the IDAC formula works well. State the purpose of the letter upfront, give the reader a brief background, include an action item, and then, close.

### IDAC (for routine and positive letters)
I: **Introduction** (main point – request for services; congratulations, etc.)
D: **Details** (explanation, reasons, background)
A: **Action** (what you expect or plan to do: meeting, phone call, delivery, etc.)
C: **Close**

For bad news letters, however, it is not a good idea to get straight to the point. You do not want to shock the recipient or reader. As such, you begin by presenting a buffer, that is, information that is neutral or positive. This will relax the reader and help serve as a lead-in to the bad news. When you deliver the bad news, please don't go into too much detail. You can soften the impact of the blow by not exaggerating the problem. Rather, you can offer another buffer after you present the bad news, and then go on to a brief close.

### BDBC: Negative situations
B: **Buffer** (say something that would soften the impact of the coming bad news)
D: **Details** (explain or give the negative news)
B: **Buffer** (give another piece of information to soften the impact)
C: **Close** (end pleasantly and briefly)

# Assignment 89

Ms Wendy Wexlinks applied for your company's Preferred Client Status Card. This card is given to very few people, usually those who have proven themselves loyal to the company for many years. The card comes with a number of perks such as free use of resorts and spas worldwide. Write to Ms Wexlinks and inform her of the approval of her application.

## Assignment 90

Mr Jimmy Hope sent you a fax: "Hello. Our printing company has installed new machines. Really good ones too. We know you have a big printing job coming up. We would really like you to offer us this job. We'll do a helluva job for you. And by the way, we need the business! Thanks."

You have been asked to reply to Mr Hope. The reality is that the large printing order has been offered to another company. You do not have any other printing jobs coming up any time soon.

# Assignment 91

| Prepositional Phrases | Form a Sentence with each of the Listed Prepositional Phrases |
|---|---|
| Be involved in | |
| Be jealous of | |
| Keep from | |
| Be known for | |
| Be limited to | |
| Be located in | |
| Look forward to | |
| Be made of | |

# Assignment 92
**Form sentences with the verbs below.**

1. liberate: _____

2. adulterate: _____

3. affect: _____

4. aggravate: _____

5. alienate: _____

6. allege: _____

7. allay: _____

8. alleviate: _____

9. allude: _____

10. alter:_____

_____

11. alternate:_____

_____

12. ameliorate:_____

_____

13. animate:_____

_____

14. antedate:_____

_____

15. appeal:_____

_____

16. appraise:_____

_____

17. praise:_____

_____

18. ascribe:_____

_____

19. excise:_____

_____

# FUN WITH GRAMMAR #18
**Choose the correct answer from the pair of italicized words or phrases.**

1. *Its/It's* going to rain.

2. I saw *me/myself* in the mirror.

3. The marketing manager is angry *to/at* the sales people.

4. I am proud *at/of* you.

5. *Hundred's/Hundreds* of birds fell from the sky.

6. I have two books. One is red, and *another/the other* is blue.

7. Some people are tall. *Another/Others* are short.

8. Mr and Mrs Tanaka love *one another/each other*.

9. The members of the basketball team teased *each other/one another*.

10. Could I *borrow/lend* your pencil for a minute? I'll return it shortly.

# Unit 19
## Holding Productive Meetings: Writing Meeting Minutes

When you attend a meeting, you might be asked to take minutes. It happens to everyone at some time. Are you confident about being able to write meeting minutes? We shall consider meeting minutes in this unit.

But first, let's consider what you'd do if you had the chance of running a meeting.

## Leading a Meeting

If you are asked to lead a meeting, there is a fairly simple way by which you can proceed.

Have an agenda and keep the following points in mind when you are introducing a topic for the first time.

a) Welcome the attendees
b) Make sure everyone has a copy of the agenda
c) Set some ground rules regarding speaking (e.g., raise your hand if you want to talk)
d) Say how long the meeting is expected to take
e) Introduce the first topic
f) Give some background on the issue for the benefit of those who may not be fully aware of what is going on
g) Say why the issue is important
h) Ask a question/seek input from others

## Lecture or Meeting?

The chairperson or the discussion leader should not talk endlessly otherwise it is not a meeting; it is a lecture.

## Meeting Minutes: Purpose

| | |
|---|---|
| • summarize discussions of a meeting | • list who attended the meeting and who did not |
| • record actions agreed upon | • serve as a reminder of decisions made |
| • take note of individual responsibilities | • serve as a historical record |

## The chairperson's role

The chairperson might want to do the following:
- follow the agenda in order to run an orderly meeting
- ask that anyone who wants to speak raise his or her hand and wait to be called upon
- make sure that everyone has a chance to express his or her ideas
- be flexible — accommodate unexpected developments
- summarize the discussion at the end of the meeting
- ensure that minutes recorded match what was said at the meeting
- use the minutes to check promised action against implementation

## The minute taker

The chairperson usually appoints one person to write down the details of the meeting. To do a good job, he or she...
- writes down the key points made at the meeting
- avoids writing down every single word
- focuses on ideas and actions, not just words
- gives copies of the minutes to attendees, including the facilitator
- gives copies of the minutes to those who were not able to attend

# Template: Taking Meeting Minutes

Subject:
Date:
Time:
Location:
Meeting Chairperson:
Attendees:
Absent:

Meeting / Discussion:

_____

_____

_____

_____

Action Item 1:               Assigned to:

Action Item 2:               Assigned to:

Action Item 3:               Assigned to:

Date Due:

Next Meeting Date:           Next Meeting Time:

Next Meeting Venue:

# Assignment 93
## Special terms pertaining to formal meetings

**Research: Find the meanings of these terms.**

| Word | Definition |
|---|---|
| Adjourn | |
| Adopt minutes | |
| Agenda | |
| Apologies | |
| Bylaws | |
| Casting vote | |
| Chairman | |
| Point of information | |
| Lie on the table | |
| Minutes | |
| Motion | |
| Opposer | |
| Point of Order | |

| Word | Definition |
|---|---|
| Other business | |
| Quorum | |
| Proposal | |
| Resolution | |
| Seconder | |
| Secretary | |
| Standing committee | |
| Table | |
| Unanimous | |

## Key points

- Minutes should not be word for word (verbatim)
- Avoid excessive detail that adds no value to the record
- Write down official decisions and actions that are mentioned at the meeting
- If the minute taker/secretary is unsure about how to express an idea, it is a good idea to voice this concern and get some suggestions from those present
- Generally, the minute taker does not actively participate in the meeting (but there is no law that says he or she cannot!)

## Types of minutes

Some styles for writing minutes are more limiting than others. Minutes can be classified into three formats:

## 1. Report style
- written in report form
- includes detailed notes on discussions (who said what, who made what motion, who seconded what motion)
- includes names of participants and their comments

## 2. Minutes of narration
- focuses on summary of main points
- commonly used in business

## 3. Minutes of resolution
- legal style that captures the exact wording of resolutions passed
- includes the names of key persons such as those who propose motions and those who second such motions
- uses active voice (Jerry Pan seconded Sarah Somme's motion)

# Assignment 94: Word Watch

| WORDS | Use each of the words below in a sentence |
|---|---|
| Breadth | |
| Breath | |
| Compose | |
| Comprise | |
| Forward | |
| Foreword | |
| Proceed | |
| Precede | |
| Appraise | |
| Apprise | |

# Assignment 95

Mr John Jinjibu, HR Director, left a voice message that you should attend a meeting tomorrow morning. Send him an email to find out what kind of meeting it is. You want to know if you should prepare some documents or if you have to make a presentation at the meeting. You are a little nervous.

Find out: a) what the meeting is about

b) if you need to prepare specially for the meeting

## Assignment 96

| Prepositional Phrases | Form a Sentence with each of the Listed Prepositional Phrases |
|---|---|
| Decide upon | |
| Decide on | |
| Be dedicated to | |
| Depend upon | |
| Depend on | |
| Be devoted to | |
| Be disappointed in | |
| Be disappointed with | |

# Assignment 97: Writing Meeting Minutes (Activity for Group Class)

Select one person to act as Chairperson and another to act as Secretary. Hold a meeting on a topic of common concern. As you go through the discussion, have the Secretary record the minutes. (You may use the meeting minutes template on page 216 or the space below).

## Assignment 98: USE YOUR THESAURUS

| | Find synonyms for CONSIDER | a. Find the exact meaning using a dictionary  b. Make a sentence |
|---|---|---|
| 1 | | a. |
| | | b. |
| 2 | | a. |
| | | b. |
| 3 | | a. |
| | | b. |
| 4 | | a. |
| | | b. |

# Assignment 99
## Form sentences with the verbs below.

1. avert: _____

2. awaken: _____

3. belie: _____

4. beset: _____

5. brandish: _____

6. bungle: _____

7. cede: _____

8. characterize: _____

9. circulate: _____

10. coerce: _____

_____

11. collide: _____

_____

12. commemorate: _____

_____

13. compare: _____

_____

14. compliment: _____

_____

15. complement: _____

_____

16. comprehend: _____

_____

17. condense: _____

_____

18. confess: _____

_____

19. confide: _____

_____

# FUN WITH GRAMMAR #19
## Choose the correct answer from each pair of italicized words.

1. The meeting is **supposing/supposed** to finish at 8 p.m.

2. The doctor would rather work than **watch/watching** a movie.

3. Lisa prefers tea **than/to** coffee.

4. He should **studying/study** this weekend.

5. The professor is **interesting/interested** in Japanese woodblock printing.

6. The school is concerned **of/about** students' poor grades.

7. The mother is worried **about/of** her son.

8. She prepared **for/on** the test.

9. The teacher is exhausted **from/for** the long hours.

10. We are interested **by/in** art.

# Unit 20
## Harvard Referencing & Citation

It is a common tradition among scholars to give credit to their sources of ideas. This system is an incentive for learners everywhere to try to contribute to the world's stock of knowledge.

Taking someone's ideas or words and representing them as your own is, in a way, stealing — also called plagiarism, a word that you do not want associated with your name.

Unfortunately, many highly accomplished writers, scholars, and businesspeople, through carelessness or laziness, have been caught using other people's words without proper attribution. Plagiarism has sunk or rattled many people's careers.

It is possible that some of those who have been accused of plagiarism were not fully aware of the rules, but, ignorance of the law is no excuse! As a businessperson or scholar, there are certain things you are expected to know. Proper citation is one of them.

For business writers, one of the referencing systems that has become quite popular is Harvard Referencing. There are many others, including, the American Psychological Association or APA format, the Modern Language Association or MLA format and the Chicago Manual of Style.

While there are similarities, each system has its supporters and each one has a detailed guide for users. The guides are also frequently updated, so look for the latest version.

Usually, the citation guide provides examples of how to cite references for various cases, for example:

- Book (with one author)
- Book (with two or more authors)
- Book with Editor, Translator, or Compiler (No author)
- Book with Author plus Editor, Translator, or Compiler
- Chapter or other part of a book
- Preface, foreword, introduction, or another such part of a book
- Electronically published book
- Article in a print journal
- Article in a newspaper or magazine
- Book review
- Paper presented at a Conference or Meeting
- Website

## Harvard Referencing

We will focus on Harvard referencing, but in your career, you may have the opportunity to use other referencing systems. Many journals have their preferences. So, if you are writing an article for a journal, you need to find out what the paper's referencing preference is.

## Google Scholar

If you find a source through Google Scholar, there is a feature called "Cite" — one of a number of links that appear under the summary of the article. The "Cite" link shows you various citations such as MLA, APA, Chicago, and Harvard. Copy the full citation you want and paste it in the reference section at the end of your report.

## Book Reference Generators

There are also many websites that take in your input (name of author, date of publication, name of journal, etc.) and generate the proper form of the citation for you. Thus, there is no excuse for not citing your sources properly.

## Harvard: Variations

Many universities and organizations have adopted the Harvard referencing system and some of them have made slight modifications to it. For example, some institutions prefer to put the date in parentheses while others prefer not to.

## Assignment 100
**Find the meanings of the following words and phrases associated with referencing and citation.**

1. bibliography: _____

2. ibid.: _____

3. footnotes: _____

4. endnotes: _____

5. in-text citation: _____

6. Alphabetical order (references): _____

_____

_____

# Assignment 101
## Find examples of Harvard Referencing for the following:

1. Book with Single Author: _____

_____

_____

2. Book with Two or Three Authors: _____

_____

_____

3. Book with No Author: _____

_____

_____

4. Journal Article (Print): _____

_____

_____

5. Journal Article (Electronic): _____

_____

_____

6. Newspaper Article (Author): _____

_____

_____

7. Newspaper article (No author): _____

_____

_____

8. Magazine article (No author): _____

_____

_____

9. Magazine article (Web - No page number): _____

_____

_____

10. Excerpt from an encyclopedia: _____

_____

_____

# FUN WITH GRAMMAR #20
**Choose the correct answer from the words in italics.**

1. The kids are **exciting/excited** about the birthday party.

2. Our company is involved **by/in** real estate.

3. I am scared **of/from** ghosts.

4. The director is tired **from/of** being ignored by her board members.

5. The artist is addicted **by/to** drinking coffee.

6. The street is crowded **in/with** young people.

7. The movie was **frightened/frightening.**

8. I was bored **on/by** the movie.

9. Thanks for **you're/your** hard work.

10. The story was **depressed/depressing.**

# Unit 21
## Summarizing

From time to time, you will be called upon to summarize or condense information.

One way to summarize is to read the article and then jot down key points from it, and from these points, rewrite the piece in your own words and at a much reduced length.

Many articles include stories, facts and figures, metaphors, and other elements that help the reader better understand the information. In your summary, you may have to leave out some of the details.

In the original, if someone writes, "James brought oranges, apples, pineapples, and bananas to the office," one word can replace the list. Can you think of it?

According to the Merriam Webster Dictionary, a summary uses a "few words to give the most important information about something."

If possible, read the original piece several times so that you have a full understanding of it. A summary that misses the point of the original is not very helpful to anyone.

## The Executive Summary

The Executive Summary of a business plan or proposal is one of the opportunities to exercise your summarizing skills. Usually, the executive summary is written after the whole report is done so that it is truly a short version of the original. It is placed at the beginning of the report.

The Executive Summary is often read by investors, potential business partners, or bank managers. These are busy people; before they commit to reading the whole report, they want to be sure that it's worth the effort.

If you are in charge of writing the summary to a business plan, you want to make sure that what the company does is answered in a way that invites the reader to continue.

Other key elements that might attract the attention of a reader are whether you have the backing of any notable people, companies, or institutions. Likewise, if your company has been able to garner a wide base of customers, this is not information that you want to keep hidden.

In addition, if you have proprietary technology that gives you and your products an edge in the marketplace, potential investors would like to know about it, both in the body of the report and in the executive summary.

In any case, any piece of writing you put your name to has to be well written, with no errors, if possible!

## Summarizing an Article

To summarize an article,

- Be sure to put down not only the writer's name but also the title of the article, and other identifying sources such as date of publication.
- Find out from the introduction to the article or from reading in-depth what the writer's purpose is.
- Write down where or how the writer got his or her information.
- Jot down key points and note examples offered by the writer.
- Note any logical connections in the writer's arguments.
- A target of one-quarter the length of the original is common, but it all depends on why you are writing the summary, who wants it, and how long the person wants it.
- A summary is not an opportunity for you to inject your own opinions, suggestions, or interpretations into a work.

**Summarize the following on page 239.**

# Multinational Enterprises (MNE)
*(by Everett Ofori/abridged from original)*

*It is eye-opening to realize that while some countries are deep in debt there are companies that have more money than whole countries. These super-rich companies are usually MNEs or Multinational Enterprises. Perhaps, because of such tremendous wealth, some people just hate big companies with a passion; the wealth of corporations, however, need not always be seen as something negative.*

*Though there are many individuals and charities around the world that have good intentions, their efforts are often weakened by the simple reality that they do not have enough money to carry out their goals. A beautiful heart alone cannot feed a child dying of malnutrition. Also, wishing for a better world when an organization is itself struggling to survive from one week to the next is no way to heal the sick and dying.*

*Many multinational corporations, on the other hand, have a lot of resources, including money and skill. As Joseph Weiss notes in the book, Business Ethics, "Because MNEs often span nations, governments, and different types of businesses and markets, their operations are based on a shared network of strategies, information and data, expertise, capital, and resources." In other words, the power of MNEs stretches across the globe and can be used for good.*

*Rather than alienating MNEs, which, whether one likes it or not, already have access to a great deal of money, would it not be better to make partners of such corporations?*

*MNEs can benefit as well from such cooperation with people and organizations that want to make the world a better place. There is a payoff for MNEs in terms of projecting a more positive image.*

*In the early days of Microsoft's rise, many people did not like the company's co-founder, Bill Gates. They complained about paying high prices for products that were not always so good. Recently, As Mr Gates has focused more and more on charitable activities, few people see Microsoft and Mr Gates in a bad light. Helping to educate children in India or protect people from malaria in Africa has recast Bill Gates as a caring soul rather than a greedy person.*

*MNEs are increasingly realizing that they can be a force for good by helping local communities. In developing countries, for example, MNEs provide jobs, and often pay slightly better than their local counterparts, thus giving families and individuals the chance for a better life than they might otherwise have had.*

*As Weiss points out, "although Nike has been criticized for its international child labor practices, it is also true that by contracting with factories abroad, it has helped employ more than half a million workers in 55 countries. Eighty three percent of Nike's workforce in Indonesia is women who would not otherwise be employed."*

*Providing job stability, training, health and safety standards in host countries can contribute to development. When such contributions become common, other companies besides MNEs may begin to introduce these elements as well in order to increase their competitiveness, and in the process, contribute to the welfare of many local workers and familes.*

**Reference**
Weiss, Joseph W. *Business Ethics: A Stakeholder and Issues Management Approach.* United States: Thomson/Southwestern, 2006.

# Assignment 102
## Summary

# Assignment 103
**Find an article on the subject of leadership or any other suitable topic. Summarize it below.**

# Assignment 104
**Find a newspaper article on the subject of robots or any other subject. Summarize it below.**

# FUN WITH GRAMMAR #21
## Choose the correct answer from each pair of italicized words.

1. The engineer is *interested/interesting* in new ideas.

2. The book was *bored/boring.*

3. I have been working hard. No wonder I am *stress/stressed.*

4. I am not sure *who/which* that gentleman is.

5. I am not sure where the clown *live/lives.*

6. It's *amazing/amazed* that some people can speak more than ten languages.

7. It's *undeniable/undeniably* that leaders are born, not made!

8. Anyone who *want/wants* to dance at the carnival is welcome to do so.

9. You may depart whenever you *desires/desire* to.

10. I said thanks to the lady *which/who* assisted me.

# Unit 22
## Reports

Reports are often necessary to inform others about a particular issue. Reports may be used to argue for a particular course of action or present the results of an investigation. Reports usually focus on a specific issue or problem, and whoever asked for the report may be in a position to do something about the problem or issue.

Determine from the outset the purpose of the report, as well as who the readers of the report might be. It is important to know if you are required to offer recommendations.

Though the person that asked for the report might have some ideas about the structure of the report, this usually falls upon the writer. A good writer will review what other writers have done and determine where he or she might keep things the same and where it might be necessary to change the approach.

A few of the reports that businesspeople may have to write include the following:

**Informational reports**
(present the facts without making recommendations or giving suggestions)

**Analytical reports**
(include both facts and analysis — may include data, explanation, narration, etc.)

**Research reports**

(involve in-depth research using qualitative or quantitative methodology and usually include literature review, data analysis, findings, and sometimes implications)

**Statutory reports**

(legal documents such as an auditor's report)

**Non statutory reports**

(non-legal reports that may be written for the benefit of policymakers, administrative planners, etc.)

**Routine reports**

(prepared for submission to management from time to time; may be helpful to management in making decisions)

**Special reports**

(incident reports, trip reports, or accident reports)

**Progress reports**

(give an account of how a project is advancing)

# A long formal report...might include the following:

## Cover letter or Memorandum:
A brief letter that introduces the report

## A Title Page:
- Short description of the report
- Date of completion/date of submission
- Author's name
- Name of organization/association
- Version of report (if applicable)

## An Executive Summary:
- A summary of the content of the report
- Useful for busy executives to get a gist of the report before committing time to read it in full

## Table of Contents:
- Shows a list of topics covered and the page numbers

## Introduction:
- Provides the reader with a context for the report
- Mentions the general subject matter, including the issue or problem that is the focus of the report
- Notes the particular questions that the report answers
- Gives a preview of the structure of the report
- Notes any limitations to the report or any assumptions made

**Conclusions:**
- Summarize key findings
- Show how the findings apply to the particular problem or issue considered
- Based on data reviewed earlier
- Do not introduce any new ideas
- Use parallel form
- Are numbered
- Use objective language

**Recommendations:**
- Provide specific suggestions to address the problem or issue presented in the report
- Present without using words like probably, maybe, or perhaps
- Introduce with a verb, for example, "Institute a program of mandatory holidays for all employees," or "Provide analysts with short breaks throughout the day"
- Present in the order of importance, for example, least important to most important or most important to least important (let the reader know which order you have chosen)

**Findings and Discussion:**
- Analyze the findings (all options): share any theories you may have used (Porter's Five Forces, SWOT (strengths, weaknesses, opportunities, threats) analysis, etc.)
- Give evidence to support your conclusions
- Provide reasons for your recommendations

**References:**
- Any information you borrow from other sources should be cited both in the text (in-text citations) and in the final reference section (in alphabetical order)
- Choose one of the common referencing styles, for example, APA (American Psychological Association); MLA (Modern Language Association) or the Harvard Referencing System (details available online)

**Appendices:**
- May include any supplementary materials that might be of interest to the reader
- Are numbered
- Are described

## A Note about Conclusions and Recommendations

Reports that place the conclusion and recommendations near the top are useful to busy executives who may not have time to read the whole report.

On the next page, you will see outlines of actual reports. They are not all the same. Though there are similarities, the content and structure are largely determined by the subject matter, how large a report needs to be written, and how detailed it ought to be.

If the report involves research, the researcher should keep track of the sources of information and give credit through in-text references or bibliography at the end of the report.

## Choose Appropriate Headings

While Introduction and Conclusion are standard, remember that as the writer you have to decide what headings are appropriate for the information you are presenting.

Break the report into logical sections or parts to help readers make their way through it.

Here are some examples of report headings:

1) TRADE MISSION REPORT — COSTA RICA

    Executive Summary
    Project Background
    Mission Objective
    Participants (Individuals)
    Participants (Companies)
    Visits & Meetings
    Conclusions
    Recommendations
    Future Activities
    Bibliography

2) JAPAN'S HEALTH CARE SYSTEM

    Executive Summary
    Introduction
    Quality Care
    Universal Care
    Affordable Care
    Government Control
    Key Lessons
    References

**SAMPLE SHORT REPORT**

**INTERNSHIP PROGRAM: AN EXAMINATION**

# Introduction

This report, written for the publisher of Cosmo Biz Magazine, Ms Luri Nagata, will examine the state of the internship program involving students from Peerless University, Seattle, Washington, USA. Every year, selected students spend three months over the summer holidays with our editorial, sales and marketing, and writing teams.

The internship program has been running for five years but this is the first report on it. This report, however, focuses only on the 20XX internship experience for which this writer has direct knowledge and information.

The four students who participated in the program in 20XX came from the Journalism and Creative Writing departments of Peerless University. As usual, they were third-year students. Their ages ranged from 18 to 21. There were two male and two female students.

# Rationale

The students participated in the internship program to learn valuable skills from the staff members of Cosmo Biz magazine. These students hoped that they would be able to apply the knowledge they acquired to their future jobs. Each intern was assigned a mentor.

# Job assignments

Interns were given the opportunity to choose a primary department. Considering that all the students were pursuing journalism or creative writing, it was important to ensure that they had tasks for which they were prepared.

Interns were given the opportunity to experience the full range of tasks including copyediting, rewriting, inputting of articles, transcribing, writing of sales letters, and interviewing. Occasionally, they were asked to write fillers and to contribute ideas for features. When the students wrote articles that were satisfactory they were given bylines.

## Cost

The agreement between Cosmo Biz and Peerless University called for the university to bear the full cost of the internship program. Interns, however, were given access to benefits available to employees such as subsidized beverages. Also, when students were sent on assignments that required going off-site, their transportation expenses were reimbursed.

## Conclusions

Staff members at Cosmo Biz appreciated the interns. The interns seemed eager to contribute and to learn, which made the experience excellent for both sides. The creative writing students appeared at times frustrated because of a seeming mismatch between their skill sets and what staff required of them at Cosmo Biz.

## Recommendations

1) The internship program should be continued as it offers benefits for both the students and Cosmo Biz.

2) It might be preferable to accept only journalism students or make sure that the creative writing students who apply are aware that the writing experience at a business magazine differs from that at a literary magazine.

3) Three students, rather than four, might be a better fit as Cosmo Biz's offices lack the space to comfortably accommodate four students along with the regular staff.

## Assignment 105: USE YOUR THESAURUS

| | Find synonyms for **PARTICIPATE** | a. Find the exact meaning using a dictionary<br>b. Make a sentence |
|---|---|---|
| 1 | | a. |
| | | b. |
| 2 | | a. |
| | | b. |
| 3 | | a. |
| | | b. |
| 4 | | a. |
| | | b. |

# Assignment 106

## Form sentences with the given verbs.

1. entertain: _____

_____

2. document: _____

_____

3. internalize: _____

_____

4. fortify: _____

_____

5. impose: _____

_____

6. influence: _____

_____

7. extend: _____

_____

8. exhibit: _____

_____

9. differ: _____

_____

10. defer: _____

_____

11. eliminate: _____

_____

12. embroider: _____

_____

13. govern: _____

_____

14. index: _____

_____

15. inspect: _____

_____

16. implant: _____

_____

17. forecast: _____

_____

18. facilitate: _____

_____

19. accord: _____

_____

# FUN WITH GRAMMAR #22

**Choose the correct answer from each pair of italicized words or phrases.**

1. Mr Kim enjoys **read/reading** books.

2. I enjoy **to play/playing** table tennis.

3. I postponed **to go/going** to the conference.

4. They considered **eating/to eat** sushi.

5. The teenagers like to **go/go to** shopping.

6. We are going **jogging/jog.**

7. We had no trouble **find/finding** the boutique.

8. Mr Oe expects **pass/to pass** the examination.

9. The dance teacher decided **close/to close** her school down.

10. The little boy admitted to **take/taking** the sugar from the bowl.

# Unit 23
## More on Reports

As you advance in your career, you may have the opportunity to write longer and longer reports. In some cases, you will do this in collaboration with others.

As noted earlier, the specific writing project you are doing will determine how the topics and headings break down. Here is another example of the table of contents for a long report.

### Self Publishing Report
I. Reasons for Self-Publishing
II. Major Self-Publishing Failures
III. Major Self-Publishing Successes
IV. Reviewing Your Area of Expertise
V. Industry Terminology
VI. Financial Matters
VII. Promotion Before Publication
VIII. Finding Your Ideal Customers
IX. Where to Sell
X. Publicity and Promotion
References

## Reminders
- Indicate who asked you to write the report.
- Categorize the material.
- Pay attention to tenses and distinguish between what is always true (simple present) and something you discovered (simple past).

SAMPLE REPORT
# DAGGOOD SECURITIES INC., TOKYO, JAPAN

REPORT ON LEARNING OPTIONS FOR STAFF

## INTRODUCTION

I was asked to investigate learning options for employees by Managing Director Estella Kumar. The following steps were followed:

1. I did some research on the Internet regarding online learning.
2. I visited 10 professional development organizations in the Tokyo area and spoke with the program managers.
3. I considered self-study manuals and hybrid models of learning.
4. I did a survey among employees.

## DISCUSSION

### Option 1: Blended Learning

Blended learning involves bringing together both independent and collaborative learning opportunities. Benefits include access to materials on e-learning platforms as well as asynchronous discussions with other learners. Access is 24/7 and materials may include audio, video, articles, and white papers. Users of an e-learning platform can save on travel costs. Blended learning provides learners with an opportunity to meet in person with subject matter experts to reinforce knowledge acquired or to clarify areas of particular difficulty.

### Option 2: Classroom

Classroom learning involves direct interaction with a facilitator, seminar leader, or instructor. Group learning in the classroom provides the opportunity for networking and for getting to know colleagues or participants from other organizations. Classroom learning also provides opportunities for instant clarification of difficult concepts.

## Option 3: Self-Paced E-learning

Self-paced e-learning involves access to a learning platform that has audio, video, articles, and quizzes. Numerous quizzes allow the learner to self-test and to track progress. There are also opportunities for discussion on bulletin boards among peers and with the instructor.

## Option 4: Self-study Manuals

Books and course materials can be made available to learners who can then go through the materials at their own pace.

## CONCLUSIONS

A survey conducted among employees regarding the four learning options above yielded the following results: Of the 146 individuals who responded, 61 expressed a preference for blended learning while 43 chose self-paced e-learning. Further, 22 people showed an interest in classroom learning while only 10 people expressed a preference for self-study.

From the above, it is clear that different employees have different learning preferences and it might be good to respect these learning choices of employees to the extent possible.

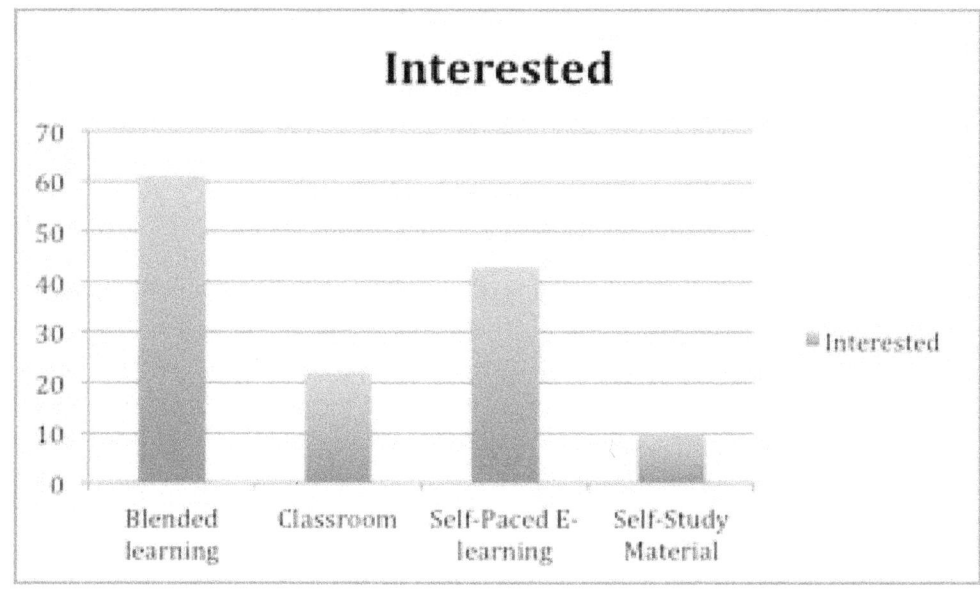

## RECOMMENDATIONS

I suggest that the company try to accommodate the preferences of learners by making all learning options available to students. This has the prospect of getting all employees to participate and to get the best benefit from the programs.

If it is necessary to choose only one or two modes of learning, then the first choice ought to be blended learning while the second should be self-paced e-learning.

James Zeffereli
Human Resources Officer

# Assignment 107
**Write a report on recent changes in your business or industry. Give your report a title.**

# Assignment 108

## Form sentences with the given verbs.

1. epitomize: _____

2. evoke: _____

3. codify: _____

4. effect: _____

5. dine: _____

6. crusade: _____

7. conceive: _____

8. excavate: _____

9. revolve: _____

10. cite: _____

_____

11. indict: _____

_____

12. humanize: _____

_____

13. furnish: _____

_____

14. expose: _____

_____

15. invert: _____

_____

16. involve: _____

_____

17. interface: _____

_____

18. grade: _____

_____

19. guard: _____

_____

20. inscribe: _____

_____

21. launch: _____

_____

22. substitute: _____

_____

23. incorporate: _____

_____

24. derive: _____

_____

25. confiscate: _____

_____

26. equalize: _____

_____

27. guide: _____

_____

28. oversee: _____

_____

28. assent: _____

_____

# FUN WITH GRAMMAR #23

**Choose the correct answer from each pair of italicized words or phrases.**

1. The nurse can't afford **buying/to buy** a house.

2. The leader failed to **facilitate/facilitating** the workshops.

3. Would you mind **coming/to come** over tomorrow?

4. The consultant advised the company to **invest/investing** in gold.

5. The secretary demanded **knowing/to know** when the letter should be mailed.

6. We **hope to/hoping** climb Mount Fuji soon.

7. Ann mentioned **to visit/visiting** Bulgaria once.

8. The diligent kid **deserved to/deserving** win the prize.

9. The inheritance allowed the little girl to **choose/choosing** her path in life.

10. The energy company **threatened to/threatening** cut off the electricity supply.

# Unit 24
## The Incident Report

Some companies have standard forms that are filled out when there is a serious incident at the workplace.

Examples of unusual events that might call for writing an incident report include the following: an accident, a fire, a fight, or an intrusion.

An incident report invariably includes a section that calls for "telling the story" of what happened. Present the information in as much detail as possible based on chronological order (First...Second...Third...Finally...).

Use transition words and connectives to help the reader make logical connections among events.

| | | |
|---|---|---|
| Before... | Earlier | First.... |
| Next... | After that... | Later... |
| Having done that... | Following that... | As soon as... |
| Shortly after that... | Just after that... | At the same time as... |
| After a while... | After about 10 minutes | Five minutes later... |
| While A was happening... | Finally... | |

## Time
after, as, before, next, during, eventually, later, finally, immediately, subsequently, soon

## Direction
above, beside, farther, nearby, opposite, elsewhere

## Addition

additionally, and, again, also, at the same time, besides, equally important, finally, further, furthermore, in addition, lastly, moreover, next

## The incident report

- Focuses on something that happened in the past
- Is written in the past tense
- Tells the story of what happened
- Is written shortly after the incident
- Summarizes the event in the order in which it occurred
- Includes the time the incident began and ended

You should start with the state of affairs before the event began. Provide details such as who was involved, what occurred, and how the incident unfolded. Did you see the events yourself or were they reported to you by someone else who was more directly involved?

If you got the information from someone else, indicate whom. What action did you take once you became aware of the incident?

## Sample Incident Report

*On August 5, 20XX, I was sitting at my desk around noon when I heard a loud noise just outside the door of the office. I walked out to check out what was wrong and found Mr Yohei Shunpei lying down – face up. He was moaning slightly. I asked him what was wrong but he just pointed to his right leg. He could not speak. I also noticed that he was not breathing properly. I shouted to the others in the office for someone to call 119. Another person joined me (it was Ms Nanami Asakura) and we knelt down by Mr Shunpei and tried to talk with him until the ambulance came. The ambulance arrived within 10 minutes and Mr Shunpei was taken away.*

# Incident Report Template

Some organizations have standard forms for reporting incidents. These vary in the number of details you have to provide but invariably there is a section for you to tell the story of what happened. Here below is a sample incident report form.

## XYZ ORGANIZATION, INC.

| | |
|---|---|
| Name/role of person filling out this form: | |
| Signature of person filling out this form: | Date: |
| INCIDENT DETAILS ||
| Date/Time of incident: | Names of people involved in the incident: |
| Description of the incident: ||
| Witnesses & their contact details:<br>a)<br>b)<br>c) ||
| REPORTING DETAILS ||
| Date on which this report is made: | Person to whom report is made: |
| Follow-up action: ||

## Assignment 109

Think of an incident that happened at work. If you have not witnessed any dramatic event, for the purpose of this assignment, use your imagination to write about something strange or unbelievable that could happen in your workplace. (Write the report as if this really happened; this would mean writing in the past tense)

Possibilities: An accident, a major disruption, equipment breakdown, breach/intrusion

_____

_____

_____

_____

_____

_____

_____

_____

_____

_____

_____

_____

_____

_____

# Assignment 110

## Form sentences with the given verbs.

1. justify: _____

_____  _____

2. pilot: _____

_____

3. pinpoint: _____

_____

4. position: _____

_____

5. preface: _____

_____

6. qualify: _____

_____

7. purchase: _____

_____

8. notarize: _____

_____

9. partner with: _____

_____

10. originate: _____

_____

11. outpace: _____

_____

12. moderate: _____

_____

13. modify: _____

_____

14. load: _____

_____

15. loan: _____

_____

16. maintain: _____

_____

17. manipulate: _____

_____

18. owe: _____

_____

19. overstretch: _____

_____

# Unit 25
## The Progress Report

Progress reports are often necessary when a company is involved in a major project such as the construction of a building, a product launch, or a marketing campaign. In such cases, it is essential to track progress, since delays can be costly.

## Key points for consideration
- Summarize your activities
- Note activities that need to be done daily
- Point out projects that you have recently started
- Highlight special efforts you have made
- Mention activities that are on hold for one reason or another
- Put down your goals and milestones

## Summary
- Introduction
- Purpose of project
- Summary of achievement to date
- Detailed description of work done (include dates)
- Cost summary (if it is your responsibility)
- Indicate if the project is still within budget (if it is your responsibility)
- Problems — and actions taken to solve them (past)
- Work scheduled for near future (with dates)
- Explanation of any potential problems and possible solutions (near future)
- Schedule of future work/tasks (with dates)
- Evaluation/Assessment of progress based on original expectations
- Estimate of date of completion of project

# Progress report sample

**SUNBIRD WEB DESIGN COMPANY**
7-11-1 Nishi-Shinjuku, Shinjuku-ku, Tokyo, Japan 160-0023 / Tel: 03-666-6666

July 1, 20XX

Ms Eleanor Kojima
Zabat Banking Group
9-3-2 Higashi-Ryouma Street
Nakano-ku, Tokyo 288-9876

Dear Ms Eleanor Kojima:

**Subject**: Progress Report #3 for June 1 to June 30, 20XX

The design of your company's website as a content management system (CMS) is progressing on schedule and within budget. Even though you made additional requests following our initial meeting, our staff have been able to devise a way to include the new requirements without your having to incur any additional costs.

**Costs**
As we indicated earlier, work by designers handling your project are billed at the rate of ¥25,000 per hour. Labor costs to date equal ¥500,000. We estimate that about 10 more hours of work, including testing, will be needed to get your website ready. This translates to ¥250,000. We have decided that this will be the ceiling and that any additional time required (if no further requests are made by your organization) will be borne by us.

**Work Completed**
As of June 30, configuration of your website is complete, with some links, content items, views, and blocks implemented. Some dummy content has also been inserted to show how the website will look once it's completed. We need to confirm how the material is displayed on a wide range of browsers, screens, and platforms, however.

**Work Scheduled**
The rest of the work will be spread over two days (July 4 & 5). Testing of all elements of the website will be done on July 5 and 6. We can confirm completion of the website and possible full online operations by July 7, 20XX.

If you have any questions or concerns, please contact me at your earliest convenience. t

Sincerely yours,

Junipa Praiss

# Assignment 111

Ms Lily Tamanja has sent your company a check for ¥490,000. She always pays her bills on time and your company is very happy with her.

Send an email to a) thank her for the payment b) invite her to the upcoming Customer Appreciation event of your company. You may want to include the date, the location where the event will be held, and the time the event starts.

## Assignment 112

**Your CEO says: "Some consultants have advised me to go on a trade mission. Research and write a short report for me to explain what trade missions are, including how we can participate in one, and if it is something that can benefit our company."**

# Assignment 113

| Prepositional Phrases | Form a Sentence with each of the Listed Prepositional Phrases |
|---|---|
| Be equipped with | |
| Escape from | |
| Excel in | |
| Excel at | |
| Be excited about | |
| Be exhausted from | |
| Excuse for | |

# Unit 26
## The Memorandum Report

The memorandum form may be used to write a short internal or interdepartmental report.

## When writing reports
- Be clear and precise
- Be factual and objective
- Use formal language

## Layout/Headings
- Use headings and subheadings
- Where necessary use numbers to clarify content
- Underline key words

A memorandum report could be any of the reports discussed earlier but presented in the form of a memo.

# Sample Memorandum Report

To:        Zogby Kohana, Marketing Director
From:      Selena Yamada, Supervisor
Date:      August 1, 20XX
Subject:   Activity Report for July 20XX

As of July 31, we are dealing with the following projects and issues.

### Projects

1. Regarding the design of websites for authors we expect to complete eight WordPress sites by August 15, 20XX.

2. We mailed out 300 books to potential reviewers, including newspapers, magazines, and bloggers. We expect to mail an additional 500 books by August 30.

3. The design of the Author Mastermind Intranet is behind schedule. We had anticipated completing it by July 31, 20XX but had to get our sole web designer, Josh Rose, into doing some database work.

### Problems

The delay in the design of the Author Mastermind Intranet stems from our having to pull our designer away from web design activities to help with mailing, data entry, and other activities. Having an extra hand in the office can help free Josh to focus on design. This will help speed up both the design of regular author websites and other design projects.

### Plans for Next Month

- Obtain a list of all bookstores in Japan
- Print 10,000 postcards featuring book covers for 10 feature authors
- Set up a Facebook page featuring our authors and their books
- Send out mailings to radio and television stations in the Tokyo area to gauge interest in featuring some of our authors

### Current Staffing Level

Current number of staff: 5
Staff request: 1

# Long memorandum report

As noted earlier, beyond the title page and the table of contents, the kind of headings you use and whether there is a recommendation section depend on the kind of report you are writing. Decide on the structure. Your knowledge of the subject matter and your general knowledge of formats should guide you to create a report that fits the purpose of the project.

**Title Page (Front page of report)**
- Title of the report and the author's name
- Date

**Contents Page**
- List sections and associated page numbers

**Introduction**
- Let the reader know the subject and the scope
- May include aims

**The Terms of Reference**
- Who was the report written for?
- What is the report about?
- When will the report be presented?

**Procedure**
- Indicate source of the information and how information was gathered

**Findings**
- Results (what did you find?)
- May include facts, figures, graphs and charts

**Conclusions**
- Summarize main points
- Recap reason for conclusion

**Recommendations**
- Indicate how the issue can be resolved
- Can be short or long-term

**Appendices**
- Additional information, usually at the back of the report; may include graphs, tables, etc.

# Assignment 115: Memorandum Report

You were assigned by the president of your company to recommend a location (hotel, hot springs resort, etc.) where senior managers can spend a week for refreshment and rejuvenation. You spent a lot of time considering different possibilities and you are now ready to present your findings, along with your recommendations.

# Assignment 116

| Prepositional Phrases | Form a Sentence with each of the Listed Prepositional Phrases |
|---|---|
| Be familiar with | |
| Feel like | |
| Fight for | |
| Be filled with | |
| Be finished with | |
| Be fond of | |
| Forgive for | |

# Assignment 117
## Form sentences with the verbs below.

1. focus: _____

_____

2. permit: _____

_____

3. overcome: _____

_____

4. generate: _____

_____

5. prevent: _____

_____

6. earn: _____

_____

7. quadruple: _____

_____

8. identify: _____

_____

9. leverage: _____

_____

10. exceed: _____

_____

11. execute: _____

_____

12. foster: _____

_____

13. enforce: _____

_____

14. reduce: _____

_____

15. gain: _____

_____

16. restore: _____

_____

17. expedite: _____

_____

18. entice: _____

_____

19. satisfy: _____

_____

# Assignment 118
## Freewriting: Ready, Set, Go!

# Unit 27
## The Trip Report

When a company pays for you to travel to participate in a conference, a business meeting, or training, the company wants to know that its investment was worthwhile.

A trip report offers you an opportunity to let the company know that they made a good decision by sending you on the trip.

**Introduction**
- Begin by stating the purpose of the trip
- Note briefly the results you obtained

**Body**
- Explain what happened, for example, the nature of the training, topics discussed, key individuals met, etc.
- Mention items that met your expectations
- Note elements that did not meet your expectations
- Provide concrete examples to illustrate your points

**Close**
- Note the benefits of the trip to the company

# SAMPLE Trip Report

**From**: Enko Lizer <enkolizer@pushpush.com>
**To**: Petro Wein <p.wein@pushpush.com>

**Subject**: Trip to New Media Marketing Seminar (Hawaii) September 28-29, 20XX

**Attachments**: Expense Report.xls (20 KB)

I attended a two-day seminar in Hawaii focusing on the use of new media to expand sales opportunities in the publishing industry.

### Presenters
The seminar featured 10 top new media marketing experts from around the world. These were not just theorists but individuals who are actively using the techniques they teach in their own highly successful businesses.

### Topics covered
- Social software
- Storytelling and narrative
- Formal specifications and data formats
- Server-side scripting languages
- Client-side scripting languages
- Asynchronous communication
- Chat programs
- New media culture
- Mobile platform

The question-and-answer session was useful and allowed me to pose some questions of particular interest to our company.

### Conclusion
Our company has been late in incorporating new media marketing techniques into our business operations. This stemmed from lack of accurate knowledge of how to proceed. Thanks to information gleaned from the new media seminar, I believe that our company can successfully implement a comprehensive program that will translate into greater awareness and sales of our products.

I will elaborate further on my experience at our next staff meeting. Meanwhile, if you have any questions, please pass them along.

Sincerely,

Enko Lizer

# Assignment 119

**If you have taken a trip in the recent past, use that information to practice writing a trip report. If not, imagine, what a work-related trip might be like and write on it.**

# Assignment 120
**Form sentences with the verbs below.**

1. trim: _____

_____

2. recommend: _____

_____

3. formulate: _____

_____

4. investigate: _____

_____

5. maintain: _____

_____

6. oversee: _____

_____

7. persuade: _____

_____

8. rank: _____

_____

9. outpace: _____

_____

10. redesign: _____

_____

11. inspire: _____

_____

12. enable: _____

_____

13. field: _____

_____

14. clarify: _____

_____

15. integrate: _____

_____

16. unify: _____

_____

17. forge: _____

_____

18. reorganize: _____

_____

18. exempt: _____

_____

# Unit 28
## The Briefing Note

Briefing notes are used to keep others up to date about the status of projects. They are commonly used among senior government officials but they are becoming popular in some business organizations.

A briefing note touches on the main points right away and involves the following steps:

### Statement of Purpose
- explain the main points of the report and why it is being written

### Background
- explain the facts and circumstances that necessitated the writing of the report
- focus on main points

### Current status
- explain how and where things stand
- point out who is involved

### Options or Next Steps
- point out any new developments
- present the information logically

# Assignment 121

Your boss wants to offer a company-wide writing program and wants to find out from your experience if taking a business writing course is worth it.

Write a report about the current writing course you are taking or about the last English course you took. Use briefing note format.

## Assignment 122: USE YOUR THESAURUS

| | Find synonyms for PREFER | a. Find the exact meaning of each word using a dictionary<br>b. Use the word in a sentence of your own |
|---|---|---|
| 1 | | a.<br><br>b. |
| 2 | | a.<br><br>b. |
| 3 | | a.<br><br>b. |
| 4 | | a.<br><br>b. |
| 5 | | a.<br><br>b. |

# Assignment 123

| Prepositional Phrases | Form a Sentence with each of the Listed Prepositional Phrases |
|---|---|
| Be friendly to | |
| Be friendly with | |
| Be frightened of | |
| Be frightened by | |
| Be furnished with | |
| Be gone from | |
| Be grateful to | |
| Be grateful for | |

# Assignment 124
**Form sentences with the verbs below.**

1. explore: _____

2. measure: _____

3. campaign: _____

4. convince: _____

5. authorize: _____

6. identify: _____

7. dispatch: _____

8. quantify: _____

9. interpret: _____

10. inspect: _____

_____

11. critique: _____

_____

12. qualify: _____

_____

13. illustrate: _____

_____

14. review: _____

_____

15. track: _____

_____

16. surpass: _____

_____

17. target: _____

_____

18. convey: _____

_____

19. define: _____

_____

# Unit 29
## Writing a Proposal

Proposals are future oriented, whereas reports often look back. Proposals are written to allow the writer or her company to present a set of ideas or plans for a reader's consideration. The proposal writer usually has the goal of swaying or persuading the reader.

Proposals may be written for any number of reasons, including the following:
- present an innovative idea
- suggest a new location for a business
- present a new way of running a plant
- suggest a new way of promoting products
- suggest a new way of running a workshop
- seek funding to conduct a study

Good proposals are well formatted, have clear headings, and may use graphics (tables, graphs, images, etc.) to tell a story that attracts the reader.

## External Proposals

Whereas some companies rely on individual consumers to buy or use their products, others depend on other companies. These are the so-called B2B relationships — business to business.

If your company relies on other companies for business, there are times when you will have to write proposals to explain how you are going to implement some program and at what cost.

## Solicited Proposals

If yours is an organization that a client has used in the past, your company's name may be on their file. If they have a project that they think you might be suitable for, they might contact you and ask you to send a proposal detailing how you plan to handle the project.

A similar request might go to other organizations that have done good work in the past. Alternatively, the company doing the soliciting might choose to advertise and request proposals from any organization that might be able to meet the terms of their request. A proposal that is requested is a solicited proposal.

## Requests for Proposals

Some big organizations, including governments, periodically advertise projects that they want to do in collaboration with the private sector. It may be a bridge that needs to be built, a dam, a recreation center, or a stadium. Usually, the government or whoever is making the request has some key requirements that proposal writers must fulfill. The request may also include key information that those interested in working on the project need to know so they can decide if it is something they want to get involved with.

In some cases, the government, or the organization making the request will post an advertisement that briefly describes the project and asks those interested to request more information or go to a website for more in-depth information.

Writing proposals for big projects often requires collaboration. Even if there is one person in charge of writing the proposal, that person may have to communicate with other people whose expertise might be necessary to complete the project.

## Assignment 125
**Write a brief email to your friend explaining what you have learned from this chapter to date.**

## Internal and External Proposals

When your company sends a proposal to another organization in the hope of getting a contract for service, that is an external proposal.

Within some large organizations, in order to make changes, ideas have to begin as proposals. In other words, those at the top are unwilling to consider ideas seriously until the ideas have been put into writing. These are internal proposals because they are generated and used within the company.

## Structure of a Proposal

The following are rough guides. The type of proposal you are writing will determine the detailed headings you include, but the following will give you an idea of the flow of ideas in a proposal.

## Sample 1

Executive Summary
Statement of Need
Project Description
Budget
Organization information
Conclusion

## Sample 2

Introduction
Current situation
Project plan
Qualifications
Cost/Benefit analysis
Budget
Conclusion

## Break it down

The idea or proposal that may be so clear in your own mind may seem confusing to others, unless you make an effort to break things down in simple, clear fashion.

One way to do this is to think about the different aspects of the proposal. For example, for a project, some of the elements that you might consider for inclusion are as follows:

## Project Description

- Concrete, specific, measurable objectives (e.g., building 5 silos)
- Conceptual (more abstract) goals (e.g., becoming a leader in the field)
- Methods: How, When, Why
- Staffing and Administration
- Evaluation
- Sustainability
- Budget (supervision, office space, materials, office overhead)
- Organizational Information

With good planning, you can work these into the general format of the proposal and help make matters clear for your reader.

# A Simple Proposal

A simple proposal might follow the conventional Introduction, Body, Conclusion format.

## Introduction
- Explain the purpose of the proposal
- Indicate how much ground you are going to cover (scope)
- Identify the key issue or issues that will be covered

## Body
- Explain what your proposal is
- Explain how you plan to implement it
- Indicate how long it is going to take (schedule)
- If applicable, indicate how much it will cost

## Conclusion
- Recap by emphasizing the key points
- Say thanks for the opportunity to share your ideas
- Note that you're willing to provide further information

# Formal Proposal (More than 5 pages)

## Design
Use headings and bullets to break up the text.

## Give the proposal a title
For example,
- An initial study
- Offer of consulting services

## Objective
State the objective of the proposal. For example,
- To identify the factors involved in......
- To examine the possibility of...
- To consider the effect of...

## Summary
The summary section presents the background of the issue and offers a number of options.

1)

2)

3)

## Proposal : Choice
This section restates one of the options, presenting it as the choice of the writer. At this point, the choice is stated briefly to prime the reader for more detailed treatment later on.

## Current Position
The position section emphasizes the current situation (in a few sentences).

## Problem
The problem section explains the effect of following in the current course. The information may be presented from the viewpoints of different stakeholders.

## Possibilities
The possibilities section expands upon the options, showing in detail the impact of each of the choices.

## Proposal : Reasons for choice
This section presents the reason for choosing a particular option.

## Appendix
If there are any appendices, please include them.

# Understand and Adapt
Though proposals have some elements in common, you will find from reading different proposals that they are not all the same. The subject matter will determine the details presented and whether it's an internal or external, solicited or unsolicited will all have a bearing on the content.

## Assignment 126

Go online and find three short proposals. Study them carefully and write a brief report detailing the similarities and differences among them. You may include what you find attractive in the proposals and what, in your view, is not so well done.

# Assignment 127

**Complete the latter part of this proposal and choose one idea as your recommended proposal.**

# Model proposal

### Memo

| | |
|---|---|
| To: | James Nakasoto, CEO |
| From: | Loran Engman, Sales Director |
| Date: | September 7, 20XX |
| Subject: | New Venue for Christmas Party |

### Introduction
We discussed the location for our next Christmas party at our sales meeting last week and you suggested that employees send their suggestions for a change of venue to me for possible consideration. I have received several ideas.

### Current Situation
For the past five years we have held our Christmas parties at our head office. This has been very convenient because the location is accessible and well known. As the company has recently relaxed rules for not only family members but friends of employees to attend the parties, the number of participants has increased considerably. This has made it impractical to continue to hold the parties at the office.

### Problem
Squeezing over a hundred people into space that accommodates only about fifty affects the quality of the party, but more importantly, it could be a fire hazard. A few employees have indicated that if the parties continue at the head office they will not attend because, in case there is an earthquake or a fire outbreak, there's bound to be a stampede.

## Proposals

The following are three possibilities:

# Assignment 128

**Your company president has invited you to submit a proposal for a project that you believe can make your company more profitable. There are no restrictions on what you can propose as long as it is an area that can be pursued successfully by the company.**

# Assignment 129

| Prepositional Phrases | Form a Sentence with each of the Listed Prepositional Phrases |
|---|---|
| Be guilty of | |
| Hide from | |
| Hope for | |
| Be innocent of | |
| Insist on | |
| Be interested in | |
| Introduce to | |
| Be involved in | |

# Assignment 130
## Form sentences with the verbs below.

1. showcase: _____

2. lobby: _____

3. demonstrate: _____

4. publicize: _____

5. compose: _____

6. survey: _____

7. outperform: _____

8. map: _____

9. assemble: _____

10. attain: _____

11. enlighten: _____

12. abdicate: _____

13. abridge: _____

14. negate: _____

15. abstain: _____

16. accede: _____

17. accept: _____

18. access: _____

19. accost: _____

# Unit 30
## Count & Noncount Nouns

The idea of count nouns in English is quite easy to grasp. Many things around you are countable: pen, shoe, pillar, label, and box, for example. These nouns have plural forms:

| **Singular** | **Plural** |
| --- | --- |
| pen | pens |
| shoe | shoes |
| pillar | pillars |
| label | labels |
| box | boxes |

These usually do not pose much of a problem. Noncount nouns, however, create problems even for some native English speakers.

Noncount nouns such as water or oil are easy enough to handle. They take the singular verb. Thus, we'd say:

*The water is hot.*
*The oil looks slick.*

Sometimes, however, the writer is not even sure whether a word is count or noncount. It is important, therefore, to review a list of common noncount nouns. They are usually classified as follows:

| Abstractions | Natural events |
|---|---|
| Activities | Materials (Solids & Semi-solids) |
| Food | Particles or Grains |
| Groups of similar items | Ailments |
| Liquids, Gases, Solids | Academic subjects |
| Languages | Words that are both Count and Noncount |

Once you get to know that a word is noncount, it is easier to know how to handle it in a sentence.

Let's begin with abstractions.

## Abstractions

| | | | | |
|---|---|---|---|---|
| advice | courage | enjoyment | fun | work |
| help | honesty | information | intelligence | time |
| knowledge | patience | art | beauty | truth |
| confidence | crime | education | experience | unemployment |
| happiness | hate | health | homework | [6]vocabulary |
| laughter | life | love | luck | patience |
| music | news | noise | nutrition | pride |
| progress | slang | peace | warmth | hospitality |
| anger | softness | justice | violence | leisure |

---

6 Vocabulary is defined by the Merriam Webster dictionary as a list of words and their meanings. The plural, vocabularies, refers to **various collections** of desired vocabulary.

# Assignment 131
**Choose five words from the list of abstractions on page 319 and form a sentence with each.**

1. _____

2. _____

3. _____

4. _____

5. _____

## Activities

| | | | |
|---|---|---|---|
| chess | homework | housework | music |
| reading | singing | sleeping | soccer |
| tennis | | | |

## Assignment 132
**Choose five words from the list above and form a sentence with each.**

1. _____

2. _____

3. _____

4. _____

_____

_____

_____

5. _____

_____

_____

_____

## Food

| beef | bread | butter | fish | toast |
| macaroni | popcorn | pork | meat | poultry |

## Assignment 133
**Choose five words from the list above and form a sentence with each.**

1. _____

_____

_____

_____

2. _____

_____

_____

_____

3. _____

4. _____

5. _____

## Groups of similar items

| | | | | |
|---|---|---|---|---|
| baggage | luggage | software | furniture | postage |
| hardware | equipment | mail | money | traffic |
| change | fruit | jewelry | junk | machinery |
| scenery | news | | | |

## Assignment 134
**Choose five words from the list above and form a sentence with each.**

1. _____

2. _____

3. _____

4. _____

5. _____

## Assignment 135
**Use each of the following words in a sentence.**

1. assess (verb): _____

2. bear (verb): _____

3. dismay (verb): _____

4. engross (verb): _____

5. vow (verb): _____

# Items of Indefinite Form: Liquids, Gases, Solids

| Liquids | Gases | Solids |
|---|---|---|
| water | steam | wool |
| tea | smoke | wood |
| soup | pollution | cheese |
| gasoline | carbon monoxide | butter |
| milk | fog | glass |
| beer | helium | salt |
| honey | oxygen | soap |
| cream | air | meat |
| juice | smog | cotton |

# Assignment 136

Choose two words from each of the three categories above and form a sentence with each.

1. _____

_____

_____

_____

2. _____

_____

_____

_____

## Natural events

| | | | | | |
|---|---|---|---|---|---|
| weather | sunshine | wind | rain | thunder | snow |
| lightning | light | darkness | heat | electricity | gravity |
| humidity | moonlight | fog | dew | fire | hail |

## Assignment 137
**Choose five words from the list above and form a sentence with each.**

1. _____

_____

_____

_____

2. _____

_____

_____

_____

3. _____

_____

_____

_____

4. _____

_____

_____

_____

5. _____

_____

_____

_____

## Materials (Solids & Semi-solids)

| wood   | wool    | lumber   | aluminum | concrete | paper |
|--------|---------|----------|----------|----------|-------|
| glue   | cotton  | concrete | cloth    | lamb     |       |
| copper | plastic | chalk    | asphalt  | brass    |       |

## Assignment 138
**Choose five words from the list above and form a sentence with each.**

1. _____

_____

_____

_____

2. _____

_____

_____

_____

3. _____

_____

_____

_____

4. _____

_____

_____

_____

5. _____

_____

_____

_____

## Particles or Grains

| | | | | |
|---|---|---|---|---|
| corn | dirt | dust | flour | rice |
| sugar | wheat | salt | hair | |

## Assignment 139
Choose five words from the list above and form a sentence with each.

1. _____

_____

_____

_____

2. _____

_____

_____

_____

3. _____

4. _____

5. _____

## Ailments

| | | | | |
|---|---|---|---|---|
| strep throat | smallpox | malaria | AIDS | rabies |
| cancer | cholera | heart disease | influenza | tuberculosis |
| flu | measles | tetanus | arthritis | |

## Assignment 140
**Choose five from the list above and form a sentence with each.**

1. _____

2. _____

3. _____

4. _____

5. _____

_____

_____

_____

## Academic subjects

| art | biology | history | psychology | economics |
| literature | engineering | music | poetry | political science |
| linguistics | physics | chemistry | mathematics | science |

## Assignment 141
**Choose five from the list above and form a sentence with each.**

1. _____

_____

_____

_____

2. _____

_____

_____

_____

3. _____

_____

_____

_____

4. _____

_____

_____

_____

5. _____

_____

_____

_____

## Languages

| French | Swahili | Russian | Spanish |
| Pampanga | Japanese | Italian | Greek |
| Hebrew | Hindi | Arabic | Romanian |

## Assignment 142
### Choose five from the list above and form a sentence with each.

1. _____

_____

_____

_____

2. _____

_____

_____

_____

3. _____

_____

4. _____

5. _____

## Words that can be both Count and Noncount

Some words may be considered count in some contexts and noncount in other contexts.

For example, you may find a hair (one strand) in your food at a cheap restaurant. In such a case, you may find yourself pulling your hair (the lot on your head) if you think you have already ingested a few strands!

A chicken (a live bird) may disturb your reading with its clucking sounds if you find yourself on a tropical island but in the nearby restaurant you may find yourself eating chicken (served as food).

Here is a list of words that can be count in one situation but noncount in another:

| | | | | | |
|---|---|---|---|---|---|
| paper | hamburger | time | life | education | crime |
| beauty | death | fire | fruit | glass | marriage |

## Assignment 143

**For each of the suggested words below, form two sentences, one in which the word is used as a count noun and the other, as noncount.**

1. Paper

a) _____

_____

b) _____

_____

2. Fruit

a) _____

_____

b) _____

_____

3. Time

a) _____

_____

b) _____

_____

4. Life

a) _____

_____

b) _____

_____

5. Crime

a) _____

_____

b) _____

_____

6. Glass

a) _____

_____

b) _____

_____

7. Death

a) _____

_____

b) _____

_____

8. Marriage

a) _____

_____

b) _____

_____

9. Fire

a) _____

_____

b) _____

_____

# Assignment 144
## Form sentences with the verbs below.

1. confront: _____

_____

2. conform: _____

_____

3. congregate: _____

_____

4. contaminate: _____

_____

5. elevate: _____

_____

6. converge: _____

_____

7. convert: _____

_____

8. curtail: _____

_____

9. defame: _____

_____

10. defraud: _____

_____

11. defray: _____

_____

12. demonstrate: _____

_____

13. demolish: _____

_____

14. deter: _____

_____

15. detest: _____

_____

16. discontinue: _____

_____

17. discover: _____

_____

18. dismiss: _____

_____

19. disregard: _____

_____

# Unit 31
# Grammatically Correct Writing

The non-native speaker who can speak grammatically correct English earns a great deal of respect. English grammar has many areas of uncertainty even for native speakers and there are many points of grammar that continue to be debated among the most learned in the English speaking world.

But your goal may not be to become a grammarian; you may just want to be able to write well enough to be understood. Bad grammar, including lack of proper punctuation, could result in misunderstanding.

If you want to be an effective business writer, you cannot afford to ignore grammar.

Grammar books sell well because many language learners recognize the importance of grammar. But once the book gets home, how often do we take the time to study it? It really does not help that many grammar books seem to try so very hard to be boring!

Still, if you are serious about improving your writing skills, you have to steel yourself to go through, not one, but several grammar books. This is because some grammar books explain some concepts better than others. So, by going through different grammar books, you may increase your chances of really getting to understand some of the more challenging areas of grammar.

Another way of improving your grammar is to become an avid reader. After all, most good writers admit to reading extensively.

# Assignment 145

| Prepositional Phrases | Form a Sentence with each of the Listed Prepositional Phrases |
|---|---|
| Be made from | |
| Be married to | |
| Object to | |
| Be opposed to | |
| Participate in | |
| Be patient with | |
| Be pleased with | |
| Be polite to | |

# Assignment 146

**Note from Headquarters: "The CEO wants all employees to be happy. Is there anything in your work life or department that you are unhappy about (e.g., too many meetings, computer crashes, etc.)? Let us know how we can make things better for you. After all, a happy employee is a better employee!"**

**Send a brief note to Employee Happiness Manager, Ms Zettai Yorokobu explaining: a) two things you are unhappy about**
       **b) what the company should do to fix the problems**

_____

_____

_____

_____

_____

_____

_____

_____

_____

_____

_____

_____

# Assignment 147

| Prepositional Phrases | Form a Sentence with each of the Listed Prepositional Phrases |
|---|---|
| Be prepared for | |
| Prevent from | |
| Prohibit from | |
| Be protected from | |
| Be proud of | |
| Provide with | |
| Be qualified for | |

# Assignment 148

**The big dictionary on the shelf near your desk has gone missing over the past two weeks. You are wondering if someone borrowed it and forgot to return it. You like that dictionary a lot and you would like to see it returned ASAP. Send an email to all employees in your branch.**

# Assignment 149

| Prepositional Phrases | Form a Sentence with each of the Listed Prepositional Phrases |
|---|---|
| Stare at | |
| Stop from | |
| Subscribe to | |
| Substitute for | |
| Succeed in | |
| Take advantage of | |
| Take care of | |
| Talk about | |

## Assignment 150

Your company has set up a series of evening courses for employees to improve negotiation skills (three hours/three nights a week). The so-called 3-3-3 (Triple Three) program will run for three weeks. You would like to see some changes made to the program because you and your colleagues are usually too tired after work to benefit fully from the program. Send an email to HR head, Mr K. Yamada, with your suggestions for change to the program.

The report, INTERNSHIP PROGRAM: AN EXAMINATION, is reproduced below. Summarize this piece on page 351.

INTERNSHIP PROGRAM: AN EXAMINATION

# Introduction

This report, written for the publisher of Cosmo Biz Magazine, Ms Luri Nagata, will examine the state of the internship program involving students from Peerless University, Seattle, Washington, USA. Every year, several interns spend three months over the summer holidays with our editorial, sales and marketing, and writing teams.

The internship program has been running for five years but this is the first report on it. This report, however, focuses only on the 20XX internship experience for which this writer has direct knowledge.

The four students who participated in the program in 20XX came from the Journalism and Creative Writing departments of Peerless University. As usual, they were third-year students. Their ages ranged from 18 to 21. There were two male and two female students.

# Discussion

The students participated in the internship program to learn some skills from the staff members of Cosmo Biz magazine. These students hoped that they would be able to apply the knowledge they acquired to their future jobs. Each intern was assigned a mentor.

# Job assignments

Interns were given the opportunity to choose a primary department. Considering that all the students came from journalism or creative writing backgrounds, it was important to ensure that they had tasks for which they were prepared. Interns were given the opportunity to experience the full range of tasks including copyediting, rewriting, inputting of articles, transcribing, and interviewing. Occasionally, they were asked to write fillers and to contribute ideas for features. When the students wrote articles that were satisfactory they were given bylines.

## Cost

The agreement between Cosmo Biz and Peerless University called for the university to bear the full cost of the internship program. Interns, however, were given access to benefits available to employees such as subsidized beverages. Also, when students were sent on assignments that required going off-site, their transportation expenses were reimbursed.

## Conclusion

Staff members at Cosmo Biz appreciated the interns, who seemed eager to contribute and to learn. The experience was fruitful for both sides. The creative writing students appeared at times frustrated because of a seeming mismatch between their skill sets and what staff required of them at Cosmo Biz.

## Recommendations

1) The internship program should be continued as it offers benefits for both the students and for Cosmo Biz.
2) It would be preferable to accept only journalism students or make sure that the creative writing students who apply for the program are aware that the writing experience at a business magazine differs from that at a literary magazine.
3) Three students, rather than four, might be a better fit as Cosmo Biz's offices lack the space to comfortably accommodate four students along with the regular staff.

# Assignment 151
## Summary

# Assignment 152
## Freewriting: Ready, Set, Go!

# Unit 32
## Additional Writing Tasks

**Assignment 153**

You are working on a presentation and need help with creating some special charts. Mr Eli Yamamura might be able to help you pull it off. Send him an urgent message asking for his assistance.

# Assignment 154

| Prepositional Phrases | Form a sentence with each of the Listed Prepositional Phrases |
|---|---|
| Be terrified of | |
| Be terrified by | |
| Thank for | |
| Think about | |
| Think of | |
| Be tired of | |
| Be tired from | |
| Be upset with | |

# Assignment 155

**Your company is considering setting up a flexible work schedule to encourage greater work-life balance. Before its implementation, however, management would like to know what each employee thinks of this idea. Email rika.honda@company.com with your views.**

# Assignment 156

The final meeting for launching your company's NextGen (next generation) services is set to begin in two hours. You have a migraine headache and might not be able to make the presentation that everyone is waiting for! Dash off a quick email to the boss, Mr Wilson Furtado, explaining your condition and predicament.

# Assignment 157

You have been informed by HR that because of your excellent work performance, you are being sent to another country for three years. You absolutely do not want to go for various reasons. You want to tell HR: "No way!!!"

# Assignment 158
**Your friend has complained to you that her boss always asks for her advice, but never follows the advice. She is getting irritated that the boss is wasting her time. You have some words of advice for your friend.**

# Assignment 159

**Your family member is seriously sick and you are the only person available to take care of her. Send an email to your boss requesting three days off.**

# Assignment 160

**Your colleague has won your company's "Employee of the Year" award. All along, you thought you would win. You are very disappointed. Send an email to congratulate your colleague.**

# Assignment 161

Your department's photocopier has broken down several times in the last few weeks. You believe that the machine will die soon and that it's probably a good idea to get a replacement. Send an email to Ms Miri Hirano, Section Head.

# Assignment 162

**Your company has a bright idea to get employees to work only four days a week by stretching the workday from 8 am to 8 pm, with a one-hour break between 12 noon and 1 pm. You are not thrilled about the idea and want to discourage the company from carrying it out. Write to the president, Ms Youngsan Park, about your concerns.**

# Assignment 163

Your boss says, "We have a number of high school students coming here tomorrow for Career Day exercises. I would like you to give them a five-minute presentation about what you like about working in this company. Send me an email explaining some of the points you intend to make in the presentation." Send to Ms Chen Ronjin.

## Assignment 164

**Try as you might, you are unable to finish paperwork before deadlines. You believe your workload is too heavy and that help from others would be a good idea. Send an email to your boss outlining why you could benefit from having an assistant.**

# Assignment 165

You have recently discovered MOOCs – massive open online courses – which offer courses in a wide variety of fields. You think your colleagues would greatly benefit from these learning opportunities. Send an email to all your colleagues informing them about these opportunities.

# Assignment 166
**Idioms Galore: Use each of the following phrases to make a sentence.**

1. ability to _____

_____

2. A rather than B _____

_____

3. accuse A of B _____

_____

4. aid in _____

_____

5. allow A to _____

_____

6. allow for _____

_____

7. amount of _____

_____

8. assure that _____

_____

9. attribute A to B _____
_____

10. based on _____
_____

11. because of _____
_____

12. believe A to be B _____
_____

13. believe that _____
_____

14. between A and B _____
_____

15. both A and B _____
_____

16. capable of _____
_____

17. choose from _____
_____

18. choose to _____

19. claim that A is B _____

20. claim to be able to _____

21. collaborate with _____

22. comply with _____

23. descend from _____

24. determined by _____

25. different from _____

26. distinction between _____

27. distinguish A from B _____

28. distinguish between A and B _____

29. doubt that _____

30. either A or B _____

31. neither A nor B _____

32. conclude that _____

33. conform to _____

34. consequence of _____

35. consider A a B _____

36. consider A B _____

37. consist of _____

38. consistent with _____

39. contend that _____

40. contrast A with B _____

41. contribute to _____

42. credit A with B _____

43. dated at _____

44. debate over _____

45. decide to _____

46. define A as B _____

47. depend on _____

48. depends on whether _____

49. X is to Y what A is to B _____

50. worry about _____

51. view A as B _____

52. unlike A, B _____

53. try to _____

54. attempt to _____

55. think that _____

56. think of A as B _____

57. sympathize with _____

58. suggest that _____

59. substitute A for B _____

60. subject to _____

61. so A as to be B _____

62. so (adjective) that _____

63. separate from _____

_____

64. same to A as to B _____

_____

65. sacrifice A for B _____

_____

66. reveal that _____

_____

67. result of _____

_____

68. result in _____

_____

69. responsible for _____

_____

70. responsibility to _____

_____

71. reluctant to _____

_____

72. regard as _____

73. range from A to B _____

74. question whether _____

75. provide with _____

76. enamored with _____

77. estimate A to be B _____

78. expend (money/time/energy/resources) on _____

79. fascinated by _____

80. for every A, B _____

81. forbid A to B _____

82. hold that _____

83. in contrast to _____

84. in contrast to A, B _____

85. in danger of _____

86. in order to _____

87. in violation of _____

88. indicates that _____

89. indifferent towards _____

90. instead of _____

_____

91. isolate from _____

_____

92. just as A, so B _____

_____

93. know A to be B _____

_____

94. know that A is B _____

_____

95. mistake A for B _____

_____

96. model after _____

_____

97. recommend that _____

_____

98. recommend you to (British English) _____

_____

99. more (adjective) than _____

100. not A but B _____

101. not only A but also B _____

102. not so much A as B _____

103. on account of _____

104. prejudiced against _____

105. in favor of _____

106. prevent A from B _____

107. prohibit A from B _____

# Assignment 167
## Use each of the following words to form a sentence.

1. apprehensive (adjective) _____
_____

2. arcane (adjective) _____
_____

3. befall (verb) _____
_____

4. burgeon (verb) _____
_____

5. coherent (adjective) _____
_____

6. compassion (noun) _____
_____

7. compassionate (adjective) _____
_____

8. compensate (for) (verb) _____

9. contour (noun) _____

10. correlate (verb) _____

11. corollary (noun) _____

12. critical (adjective) _____

13. cumbersome (adjective) _____

14. deficit (noun) _____

15. demean (verb) _____

16. variable (noun) _____

_____

17. uniform (adjective) _____

_____

18. trial (noun) _____

_____

19. solution (noun) _____

_____

20. residual (adjective) _____

_____

21. precipitation (noun) _____

_____

22. onset (noun) _____

_____

23. maturation (noun) _____

_____

24. mass (noun) _____

25. latter (noun) _____

26. interval (noun) _____

27. intact (adjective) _____

28. incremental (adjective) _____

29. given (adjective) _____

30. generalize (verb) _____

31. fuse (verb) _____

32. exert (verb) _____

_____

33. evolution (noun) _____

_____

34. erode (verb) _____

_____

35. emit (verb) _____

_____

36. efficient (adjective) _____

_____

37. decelerate (verb) _____

_____

38. deposition (noun) _____

_____

39. characteristic (adjective) _____

_____

40. altitude (noun) _____

41. abundant (adjective) _____

42. wholly (adverb) _____

43. void (verb) _____

44. trivial (adjective) _____

45. trait (noun) _____

46. characteristic (noun) _____

47. skeptical (adjective) _____

48. rudimentary (adjective) _____

_____

49. revive (verb) _____

_____

50. relevant (adjective) _____

_____

51. resent (verb) _____

_____

52. profound (adjective) _____

_____

53. principle (noun) _____

_____

54. predate (verb) _____

_____

55. ponder (verb) _____

_____

56. perpetual (adjective) _____

_____

57. peril (noun) _____

_____

58. pensive (adjective) _____

_____

59. omit (verb) _____

_____

60. omission (noun) _____

_____

61. notion (noun) _____

_____

62. nostalgia (noun) _____

_____

63. mere (adjective) _____

_____

64. lethargic (adjective) _____

_____

65. latent (adjective) _____

_____

66. justify (verb) _____

_____

67. integrate (verb) _____

_____

68. infer (verb) _____

_____

69. inevitable (adjective) _____

_____

70. inconceivable (adjective) _____

_____

71. incompetent (adjective) _____

_____

72. incendiary (adjective) _____

73. impervious (adjective) _____

74. imminent (adjective) _____

75. glaring (adjective) _____

76. devoid (adjective) _____

77. digress (verb) _____

78. diminish (verb) _____

79. discrepancy (noun) _____

80. adjust (verb) _____

_____

81. diminish (verb) _____

_____

82. disposition (noun) _____

_____

83. dynamic (adjective) _____

_____

84. eclipse (verb) _____

_____

85. eminent (adjective) _____

_____

86. reprise (verb) _____

_____

87. inconsequential (adjective) _____

_____

88. roil (verb) _____

_____

89. malleable (adjective) _____

_____

90. unconscionable (adjective) _____

_____

91. retentive (adjective) _____

_____

92. foist (verb): _____

_____

93. countermand (verb): _____

_____

94. protest against (verb): _____

_____

## Assignment 168
**You think that an employee suggestion box will help improve your company's overall practices, and perhaps, profits. Share the potential benefits of having a suggestion box with your colleagues.**

# Assignment 169

You are the boss. Times are hard and you are forced to do the unthinkable: reduce employee salaries. You think this will be temporary and you find no joy in having to do it but the company may not survive otherwise. Send an email to all employees informing them about the company's current situation and the plan you have come up with to keep the company afloat.

# Assignment 170

**A former employee, Ms Sayaha Balbadur, has asked you to write a letter of recommendation extolling her professional virtues, experience and contributions to your firm. Write the letter with the following attention line: To Whom It May Concern**

# Assignment 171

**You made an inexcusable mistake at work for which you have apologized in person to your colleagues. You feel, however, that an email apology as a follow-up will allow you to express more fully the sincerity of your apology. Send an email to your colleagues affirming your regret for the unintended error and assuring them that such a mistake shall never occur again.**

# Assignment 172

**You recently interviewed two applicants for a position in your company. You were impressed with the overall background and skills of both applicants. Unfortunately, there was room for only one hire. Send an email to the applicant who was not hired.**

# Assignment 173

**You are inspired by the accomplishments of scientists – their dedication, willpower, curiosity, and willingness to collaborate with others. You want employees in your company to develop similar qualities. Write an email to a Nobel Prize winner of your choice and invite her to give the keynote address at your company's end-of-year function.**

## Assignment 174

Your boss says, "Please do some research on the correct use of LESS and FEW for the benefit of employees. Present your results to me in the form of a report. Cite your sources."

## Assignment 175

**Your boss says, "Please do some research on the use of NONE and NEITHER for the benefit of employees. Present your results to me in the form of a report. Cite your sources."**

# ANSWERS TO FUN WITH GRAMMAR QUIZZES

### FUN WITH GRAMMAR #1
1) Yesterday, I sent the parcel.
2) I recognize that the Internet is critical to business.
3) The Asian Tiger countries produce a lot of technology products.
4) Every February, we go to Hokkaido.
5) Right now, I do not have any plans to take a vacation.
6) I have brought some chopsticks with me.
7) Last week, he broke his leg.
8) The business has grown a lot in the last few months.
9) He spoke very well at the conference last month.
10) She wore a kimono to the picnic last Saturday.

### FUN WITH GRAMMAR #2
1. After she writes the article, I will send it to the editor.
2. Before he leaves, we will visit the zoo.
3. After we ate last night, we went immediately to the meeting.
4. Tomorrow, I will prepare some slides for the boss.
5. By the time I finish the project, she would have returned.
6. If you want to know more you must read more.
7. You can meet interesting people anywhere you go.
8. Right now, the boss is dozing in his office.
9. Currently, I'm reading a book by Inazo Nitobe.
10. Have you seen the latest Harry Potter movie?

### FUN WITH GRAMMAR #3
1. The clerk *pored* over the document.
2. The supermarket *aisle* was full of carts.
3. On our visit to Morocco, we went to a *bazaar*.
4. The marketing manager *broached* the subject of social media to the CEO.
5. Telemarketing can be a *complement* to other forms of advertising.
6. If you *flout* too many rules on the job, you will be let go.
7. The president spoke in a monotone; I was so *bored*.
8. Many accidents are *preventable*.
9. Everybody wants to *succeed*.
10. Sometimes, businesspeople have to be *patient*.

### FUN WITH GRAMMAR #4
1. The sky is blue. (be)
2. Jamie always goes to the gym after work. (go)
3. Baby seals are cute. (be)
4. Office ladies adore Hello Kitty. (adore)
5. The chef makes chocolate pie every week. (make)
6. The chef's apprentice made blueberry scones last week. (make)
7. Few babies have thirty-two teeth. (have)
8. I have known that guy since elementary school. (know)
9. They eat a lot of mangoes every year. (eat)
10. She works late into the night each day. (work)

## FUN WITH GRAMMAR #5
1. The United Nations *is* working to make the world a peaceful place.
2. The United States *is* still a leader in world affairs.
3. Five hours of sleep *is* not enough for me.
4. The Irish *love* coffee.
5. Japanese *is* the language of my heart.
6. One and one *is* two.
7. Five dollars *is* enough to buy a bowl of noodles.
8. The police *are* good at giving directions.
9. The news this morning *is* not good.
10. Linguistics *is* interesting.

## FUN WITH GRAMMAR #6
1. Every child *needs* attention.
2. The population of India *is* over 1 billion.
3. Each of my friends *reads* one book a week.
4. One of the most challenging problems today *is* global warming.
5. Both boys and girls *are* capable of learning complex concepts.
6. Three hours *is* too much for making an omelet.
7. A red and yellow rabbit *is standing* on the desk.
8. Almost half of the land *is* covered with water.
9. Eating too much chocolate *is* bad.
10. A red rabbit and a yellow rabbit *sit* on the chair every day.

## FUN WITH GRAMMAR #7
1. Two men are standing on the roof. (man)
2. Human beings have thirty-two teeth. (tooth)
3. Sandwiches are easy to prepare. (sandwich)
4. Knives should be stored properly. (knife)
5. Some people use washing machines to clean potatoes . (potato)
6. What are the criteria for selecting astronauts? (criterion)
7. The school is trying out various curricula / curriculums. (curriculum)
8. Radios are very useful for people who are isolated. (radio)
9. In Japan, photos are required of job applicants. (photo)
10. Pharmaceutical researchers find mice very useful in their work. (mouse)

## FUN WITH GRAMMAR #8
1. The chair fell on the manager's leg.
2. My uncle's son is my cousin.
3. The company specializes in ladies' watches.
4. The boss' wife is an engineer.
5. A diplomat's work sounds exciting.
6. The speaker's bureau has a list of 100 motivational speakers.
7. Children's books can be a lot of fun to read.
8. The professor's arm got caught in the swing.
9. My wife's ball gown looks splendid.
10. Akiko's plan was accepted.

**FUN WITH GRAMMAR #9**
1. Every singer knows the value of good breathing techniques.
2. Cooking has become popular among businesspeople.
3. Statistics is my favorite subject.
4. A lot of the equipment on the construction site is useless.
5. The number of tables needed is ten.
6. A number of scientists are working on a cure for cancer.
7. Each player has a jersey.
8. Each of the marathon runners deserves praise.
9. Most of the children's homework is badly done.
10. Statistics are often used to lie to people.

**FUN WITH GRAMMAR #10**
1. It is obviously a computer error.
2. Airplane pilots must be able to react quickly.
3. Computer skills are becoming more and more important.
4. I took a three-hour examination last Friday.
5. Lily has a seven-year-old brother.
6. Dr Finkelstein is a university professor.
7. Dr Kimiko Ogawa is a teacher's teacher.
8. A five-hour flight is not so bad.
9. I have fifteen years' experience as an editor.
10. Taxi drivers in London apparently have bigger brains!

**FUN WITH GRAMMAR #11**
1. Mrs Bella Balala is a competent manager.
2. Mr Kinjo is delighted with his new position.
3. She was delighted to meet me.
4. The caterer apologized for the mixup.
5. Lennox enjoys reading business books.
6. The head office is opposite the theatre.
7. Ms Pinto quite likes her job.
8. While the technician was speaking, someone took a picture.
9. There was no evidence that the company had committed any crime.
10. She must have completed her preparations for the summer.

**FUN WITH GRAMMAR #12**
1. Some of the clothing in the bag is good.
2. Mathematics is as much fun as grammar.
3. Very few schools use chalk today.
4. The evidence is insufficient.
5. Laughter is the language of love.
6. American slang is fun to listen to.
7. Most babies have no hair.
8. Intelligence is not only about solving problems on paper.
9. I got a lot of advice from friends.
10. Patience is often necessary for patients.

## FUN WITH GRAMMAR #13
1. The design was especially clever.
2. Putting all your cards on the table in a negotiation puts you at a disadvantage.
3. It is not advisable to work for several days without sleep.
4. The vendor was very apologetic after delivering the wrong products.
5. It is always a challenge to choose among several excellent candidates.
6. It is unwise to make a habit of fighting with everyone at the office.
7. Some companies exist for the sole purpose of imitating others.
8. Businesses should be aware of both opportunities and threats.
9. Every company should take an interest in the professional growth of its employees.
10. How a company differentiates itself from others is critical.

## FUN WITH GRAMMAR #14
1. We bought some furniture for the room.
2. The scenery on that mountain road is incredible.
3. The teacher gave us a lot of homework.
4. The kid has a large vocabulary.
5. There is too much information today.
6. We need to get new machinery.
7. Oranges are great for making drinks.
8. We should reduce the amount of garbage in the landfills.
9. Studying is a lot of fun.
10. Beauty is almost always welcome anywhere.
11) There are many people in the conference room.

## FUN WITH GRAMMAR #15
1. Our delay made the customers very angry.
2. Some people draw strength from failure.
3. Scientists are saying that intelligence is important, but so is emotional stability.
4. It is miserable when you go camping and it rains nonstop.
5. The ease with which she untied the knot left everyone stunned.
6. Being happy is a choice.
7. There is nothing wrong with being a little adventurous.
8. Being too cautious can be costly in business.
9. If you are determined enough, you can achieve almost anything.
9. It is always exciting to win a prize.

## FUN WITH GRAMMAR #16
1. It is encouraging to see so many young people striving to achieve their goals.
2. There are some gorgeous artworks in the Tokyo National Museum.
3. Being nervous before a speech is quite normal.
4. An office that is spotless gives a good impression to clients.
5. Deliberately manipulating others is repulsive.
6. You will get a puzzled look when you ask difficult questions.
7. Many people get upset when they get criticized.
8. The company president bellowed: "I am proud of you all."
9. It is outrageous for people to throw litter on the street.
10. The speaker put her notes on the lectern and began her speech.

### FUN WITH GRAMMAR #17
1. The CEO asked us what was at stake.
2. We were asked to provide a ballpark figure.
3. After the meeting, the chairperson said: "Let's call it a day!"
4. We realized shortly after the launch that we had made a mistake and that we needed to cut our losses.
5. When it comes to ethics, there are so many gray areas.
6. Many supervisors want to be kept in the loop about what is going on in the company.
7. When a relationship just doesn't work it is best to sever ties.
8. The new recruit managed to talk the manager out of implementing the sales campaign.
9. Whether we will open a new branch in China is all up in the air.
10. The best form of advertising is said to be word of mouth.

### FUN WITH GRAMMAR #18
1. It's going to rain.
2. I saw myself in the mirror.
3. The marketing manager is angry at the sales people.
4. I am proud of you.
5, Hundreds of birds fell from the sky.
6. I have two books. One is red, and the other is blue.
7. Some people are tall. Others are short.
8. Mr and Mrs Tanaka love each other.
9. The members of the basketball team teased one another.
10. Could I borrow your pencil for a minute? I'll return it shortly.

### FUN WITH GRAMMAR #19
1. The meeting is supposed to finish at 8 p.m.
2. The doctor would rather work than watch a movie.
3. Lisa prefers tea to coffee.
4. He should study this weekend.
5. The professor is interested in Japanese woodblock printing.
6. The school is concerned about students' poor grades.
7. The mother is worried about her son.
8. She prepared for the test.
9. The teacher is exhausted from the long hours.
10. We are interested in art.

### FUN WITH GRAMMAR #20
1. The kids are excited about the birthday party.
2. Our company is involved in real estate.
3. I am scared of ghosts.
4. The director is tired of being ignored by her board members.
5. The artist is addicted to drinking coffee.
6. The street is crowded with young people.
7. The movie was frightening.
8. I was bored by the movie.
9. Thanks for your hard work.
10. The story was depressing.

**FUN WITH GRAMMAR #21**
1. The engineer is interested in new ideas.
2. The book was boring.
3. I have been working hard. No wonder I am stressed.
4. I am not sure who that gentleman is.
5. I am not sure where the clown lives.
6. It's amazing that some people can speak more than ten languages.
7. It's undeniable that leaders are born, not made!
8. Anyone who wants to dance at the carnival is welcome to do so.
9. You may depart whenever you desire to.
10. I said thanks to the lady who assisted me.

**FUN WITH GRAMMAR #22**
1. Mr Kim enjoys reading books.
2. I enjoy playing table tennis.
3. I postponed going to the conference.
4. They considered eating sushi.
5. The teenagers like to go shopping.
6. We are going jogging.
7. We had no trouble finding the boutique.
8. Mr Oe expects to pass the examination.
9. The dance teacher decided to close her school down.
10. The little boy admitted to taking the sugar from the bowl.

**FUN WITH GRAMMAR #23**
1. The nurse can't afford to buy a house.
2. The leader failed to facilitate the workshops.
3. Would you mind coming over tomorrow?
4. The consultant advised the company to invest in gold.
5. The secretary demanded to know when the letter should be mailed.
6. We hope to climb Mount Fuji soon.
7. Ann mentioned visiting Bulgaria once.
8. The diligent kid deserved to win the prize.
9. The inheritance allowed the little girl to choose her path in life.
10. The energy company threatened to cut off the electricity supply.

# References

Buffett, Warren. Annual Report 2006. Berkshire Hathaway.

Interviews. Ernest Hemingway, The Art of Fiction, No. 21, *The Paris Review* www.parisreview.org

Taylor, Shirley. Model Business Letters, E-mails & Other Business Books. 6th Edition. Pitman Publishing Co., 2003

# Recommended Books

Bradbury, Ray. Zen in the Art of Writing. New York: Bantam, 1992.

Burchfield, Robert William, ed. The new Fowler's modern English usage. No. RD C10 10. Oxford: Clarendon Press, 1996.

Flesch, Rudolf Franz. "Art of readable writing." (1949).

Flesch, Rudolf. "The art of clear thinking." (1951).

Schrampfer Azar, Betty. "Understanding and using English grammar." Published by Binarupa Aksara (1999).

Strunk, William. The elements of style. Penguin, 2007.

Swan, Michael. Practical english usage. No. 425 S926P 1995.. New-York, 1992.

Waddell, Marie L. The art of styling sentences: 20 patterns for success. Barron's Educational Series, 1993.

*\* These are just suggestions to give you an idea of the kind of books you should look for if you are eager to improve your writing and grammar.*

## About the Author

Everett Ofori holds an MBA from Heriot-Watt University (Scotland, UK). He teaches Public Speaking, Management, Marketing, and English for Specific Purposes (Business Writing, Medical Writing, Meeting Facilitation, etc.). He has worked extensively with business executives (including those at the C-level) but is equally at home with helping young people hone their writing skills or become more effective in expressing themselves verbally. Everett has helped hundreds of high school and university students around the world to improve their writing and grades.

Everett has worked with clients/students from the following organizations and more:

| | |
|---|---|
| • Accenture | • Actelion |
| • Asahi Kasei Medical | • Asahi Soft Drink Research, Moriya |
| • Barclays | • Becton Dickinson |
| • Boston Consulting | • Coca Cola |
| • Deutsche Bank | • Disney Japan |
| • ExxonMobil | • Fujitsu |
| • Goldman Sachs | • Hitachi Design |
| • IIJ (Internet Initiative Japan) | • Johnson & Johnson (Janssen) |
| • McKinsey Japan | • Mitsubishi (Shoji) |
| • Mizuho Bank | • Moody's |
| • National Institute of Land and Infrastructure Management, Tsukuba, Japan (NILIM) | • Nomura |
| • Orix | • PriceWaterhouseCoopers (PWC) |
| • Recruit | • Reinsurance Group of America (RGA - Japan) |
| • Sekizenkai Nursing School, Shimosoga, Kanagawa | • Sumitomo |
| • Summit Agro International | • Suntory |
| • Tokyo International Business College, Asakusabashi, Tokyo | • Yahoo (Gyao) |
| • Yokogawa Meters and Instruments | • Yokohama Child Welfare Vocational College (Hoiku Fukushi), Higashi Totsuka, Kanagawa |

www.ingramcontent.com/pod-product-compliance
Lightning Source LLC
Chambersburg PA
CBHW081103080526
44587CB00021B/3429